Bob Dylan
The Illustrated Biography

Bob Dylan

The Illustrated Biography

CHRIS RUSHBY

Welcome Rain Publishers New York

This Edition Published by Welcome Rain Publishers LLC in 2009

First published by
Transatlantic Press
38 Copthorne Road
Croxley Green, Hertfordshire
WD3 4AQ, UK

© Transatlantic Press
For photograph copyrights see page 224

ISBN 1-56649-999-2 / 978-1-56649-999-6

Printed and bound in Malaysia

Contents

Introduction

Bob Dylan is a unique artist: writer of some of the most memorable popular songs of the twentieth century ("Like a Rolling Stone", "Blowin' in the Wind", "All Along the Watchtower") as well as a charismatic performer and cultural influence on succeeding generations of audiences and artists. Yet Dylan remains an enigma: a shy, retiring man who hardly speaks to audiences, yet now hosts a weekly radio show; a performer who, in his own words, is "mortified" to go out on stage, yet continues a punishing tour schedule in his seventh decade because he believes it's what he was born to do.

Bob Dylan was born Robert Allen Zimmerman on 24 May 1941 in Duluth, Minnesota. His early years were spent in a conventional and middle-class Jewish household. In his teens, Dylan began to play and sing in local bands and when he left school his main ambition, as recorded in his high school yearbook, was "to join Little Richard". But it was folk, not rock 'n' roll, which gave the young Dylan his first taste of fame when he moved to New York, became part of the burgeoning folk music scene and recorded a series of albums cementing his place as a leading light of the early sixties protest movement.

In 1965 Dylan famously "went electric" at the Newport Folk Festival, outraging purist fans, but finding a new and ever growing rock audience. Dylan toured the world with a rock backing band, creating music of an intensity never heard before in pop music, once again outraging some fans and thrilling others with the power of these performances.

A mysterious motorcycle accident put paid to the touring in 1966 and Dylan retired to Woodstock to raise a family. It was not until 1974 that he returned to touring and began to make great music again, notably the *Blood on the Tracks* album, which many consider to be his finest. In 1979 Dylan was "born again" and made several albums of overtly Christian music, yet again dividing his fans. Through the 1980s Dylan struggled to find his way musically and personally, although embarking on what has since become known as the Never Ending Tour: a punishing schedule of touring around the world, unprecedented in size and scope, all the more surprising for a man of his age.

The 1990s saw another creative renaissance and Bob Dylan today has rarely been more feted critically and commercially. His last three albums have been acclaimed, his autobiography *Chronicles* was both a critical and a popular success, and his *Theme Time Radio Hour* radio show a joy to fans and new listeners alike. And the Never Ending Tour continues ...

Part One

Freewheelin'

The young folk troubadour

Opposite: The young Dylan arrived in New York early in 1961, having begun to learn his craft in rock 'n' roll bands while at school; and on the folk circuit while at university in Minneapolis. Dylan was soaking up musical influences and already starting to write his own songs, drawing heavily on the folk tradition.

Above: Dylan in a pose reminiscent of folk singer Woody Guthrie, one of his early idols. Guthrie's autobiography *Bound For Glory* had captivated Dylan, as did songs like "This Land Is Your Land". Soon after arriving in New York Dylan visited Guthrie, by now hospitalized with the Huntington's Chorea which was eventually to kill him. The frail Guthrie was pleased to have Dylan sing him his own songs in a voice drawing heavily on Guthrie's own vocal mannerisms and styling.

Cafe Wha?

Opposite: Dylan in February 1961 at the Café Wha? in Greenwich Village. Dylan is seen performing with fellow folk singers Karen Dalton and Fred Neil (who later found fame writing the song "Everybody's Talkin'" for the film *Midnight Cowboy*) and (left) playing guitar and harmonica.

Early performances

Opposite: The photograph used in the flyer advertising Dylan's first true professional gig in New York, supporting John Lee Hooker at Gerde's Folk City, April 11, 1961. The young performer had been casting around for a more appropriate stage name and by the time he arrived in New York Robert Zimmerman had become Bob Dylan. There are several different versions of how the name came about, but the consensus is that Dylan Thomas, the Welsh poet whose work Dylan much admired at the time, was the main influence on the choice.

Left: Dylan slowly built a reputation in the folk scene and made friends with influential performers such as Dave van Ronk and Pete Seeger. Living in Greenwich Village, he played the folk circuit in clubs there like the Gaslight and Gerde's, strumming an acoustic guitar and blowing a harmonica fastened round his neck in a metal harness he'd made himself. Not everyone in the folk scene could see Dylan's talent and not everyone liked his voice, but Dylan persevered and his star began to rise.

Bob and Suze

Opposite and right: An uncharacteristically cheerful Dylan and his then girlfriend Suze Rotolo, photographed in their apartment in Greenwich Village. Although silent for many years about their relationship, Rotolo's recently published autobiography records this period in their lives as a time of happiness and creativity. She was one of the early loves of Dylan's life and inspired some of his most touching love songs of the time.

Suze's mother was unhappy with Dylan and his daughter as an item and encouraged her to take the opportunity to study in Italy. Their separation prompted Dylan to write some of his best love songs of the time including "Boots of Spanish Leather".

The first album

Opposite: Dylan recording his first album in New York in November 1961. Dylan had been 'discovered' by Journalist Robert Shelton, who watched the show Dylan gave supporting John Lee Hooker and wrote a landmark review of it, praising the "distinctive folk stylist" and bringing him to the attention of a wider audience, including CBS producer John Hammond.

Right: The first album, *Bob Dylan*, contained just two Dylan original songs: "Song to Woody" (a homage to his early idol) and "Talkin' New York." The other songs were folk and blues standards from Dylan's repertoire in the folk clubs. By the time the album was released some months later Dylan had already moved on, was writing more of his own songs and was dissatisfied with the selection on the album.

Hammond's folly

Above: Dylan and his first producer, John Hammond, in the studio recording Dylan's first album. CBS producer Hammond signed Dylan to Columbia, having previously discovered Billie Holiday and worked with Benny Goodman and other famous artists. The first album was not a commercial or critical success and Dylan quickly became known as 'Hammond's folly' amongst cynical CBS executives

Right: Hammond produced the first album, capturing the folk sound of Dylan, his guitar and harmonica over just two days in the studio in New York. Amongst the songs Dylan included on the album was "House of the Rising Sun" which would become a hit for the Animals two years later. Dylan's voice on this album, a gruff, strange folk blues instrument, has divided fans and critics then and now for more than 40 years. Dylan once claimed to be "just as good a singer as Caruso... You have to listen closely... but I hit all those notes. And I can hold my breath three times as long if I want to."

Performing in a play

Opposite and left: Late in 1962, Dylan visited the UK for the first time, hired by the BBC to perform in a TV play called *Madhouse on Castle Street*. Dylan made contact with performers from the English folk scene, including the young Martin Carthy, and performed at London clubs such as the Troubadour.

Madhouse on Castle Street features Dylan as a young folk singer and is most notable for an early performance of what was to become one of his most famous songs, "Blowin' in the Wind". Sadly, the tapes of the play were later wiped by the BBC and what would have been a landmark early TV appearance by Dylan is thought no longer to exist as a recording.

Politics and protest

Left: Dylan reads a spoof "War Declared" headline in a student newspaper. The early 1960s saw America and the world in political and social ferment: Kennedy as president, the Bay of Pigs, the Cuban Missile Crisis, the growing conflict in Vietnam, racism and civil rights marches at home; and Kennedy's assassination. Dylan's song-writing of the time provides a soundtrack for these momentous times and he became a hero to millions who believed music could help them build a better world.

Opposite: Dylan pictured in the studio. At this time Dylan came to be managed by the mercurial Albert Grossman, in some ways the Colonel Tom Parker to Dylan's Elvis. Grossman already managed folk acts like Peter, Paul and Mary and seemed always able to spot and nurture talent. Although always his own man, Dylan benefited from Grossman's shrewd business sense and the two prospered together.

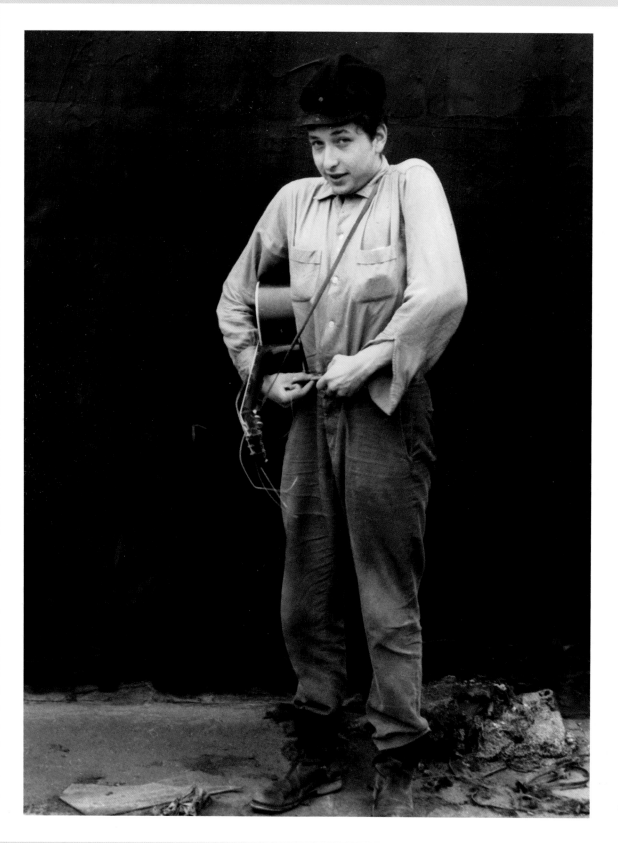

Freewheelin'

Left: Huck Finn, Charlie Chaplin and Woody Guthrie seem rolled into one in this image. Dylan was writing prolifically by now and continuing to perform in New York and elsewhere. The songs for his second album were being written and tried out in live performance.

Opposite: *The Freewheelin' Bob Dylan*, released in May 1963, was Dylan's second album and the one that brought him to a wider audience than the folk purists. Apart from "Blowin' In The Wind" (soon to be turned into an international hit by Peter, Paul and Mary) the album contains classic Dylan tracks such as "A Hard Rain's a-Gonna Fall", "Masters Of War" and "Don't Think Twice, It's Alright".

The king and queen of folk

Opposite: Dylan and Joan Baez performing in 1963. Baez, already an established and much-loved performer on the folk scene, was not impressed with Dylan at first, calling him "grubby beyond words" after their first meeting at Gerde's Folk City. Nevertheless, both their personal and creative relationships blossomed, Baez helping Dylan's career significantly by bringing him on stage to sing duets with her at a time when she was by far the better-known artist.

Right: Dylan – young folk heart-throb. Dylan and Baez performed at the Newport Folk Festival in 1963 to huge audience acclaim. They closed the festival, along with Peter, Paul and Mary, Pete Seeger and others, singing "We Shall Overcome" and Dylan's "Blowin' In The Wind", by now a hit record and as much of an anthem for the folk movement as any of its traditional favourites.

Growing fame

Opposite: Dylan continued to perform, both with Baez and as a solo act. His fame grew, he was interviewed by *Newsweek* and performed for the first time at Carnegie Hall. At this time he was widely seen as "spokesman for the young" and the representative of a disaffected, politically left-of-centre generation.

Right: After the success of *The Freewheelin'* Dylan began to write the material that would eventually surface on his next album *The Times They Are a-Changin'* early in 1964. Producer Tom Wilson had by this time replaced John Hammond, who did not see eye to eye with Albert Grossman about where Dylan's music should be going.

The protest movement

Above: Dylan and Joan Baez at the 1963 Civil Rights March on Washington, one of the landmark moments in the campaign for black emancipation in the United States. Dylan, along with Baez and numerous other famous artists, performed essentially as a warm-up act for Dr Martin Luther King: this was the day King was to deliver his famous "I have a dream..." speech and Dylan's reputation was further enhanced by the appearance.

Opposite: 8 August 1964, New York City: Dylan poses for a portrait that appears on the cover of his *Another Side of Bob Dylan* album.

The Ed Sullivan Show

Opposite and above: Dylan rehearses for *The Ed Sullivan Show*, May 1963. This was set to be his first national TV appearance and in rehearsal Dylan performed a song called "Talkin' John Birch Paranoid Blues", poking fun at the extreme right-wing John Birch Society and the communist witch-hunt mentality associated with it. When the CBS executives told Dylan the song was unacceptable and that he should substitute something less controversial he walked out of the session, asserting that he would perform this song or nothing at all. The walk-out only enhanced Dylan's reputation within the folk-protest movement.

Changing times

Above: Dylan and Baez would continue to perform together on and off for many years, although their close relationship was becoming strained by Dylan's relationships with other women. To this day, Baez sings Dylan songs in performance and does a mean impersonation of her one-time lover. In No Direction Home, Martin Scorsese's powerful Dylan documentary, Dylan himself makes a rare, revealing comment on the subject to the interviewer when asked about the difficulties of his time with Baez, saying "you can't be wise and in love at the same time", the nearest he has ever come to acknowledging their closeness.

Opposite: In June 1964 he recorded the songs for his next album, *Another Side of Bob Dylan* in a single remarkable night of recording with Tom Wilson in New York. The album was released in August and contained classic Dylan tracks such as "It Ain't Me Babe", "Chimes of Freedom" and "My Back Pages". This album marks a move by Dylan away from his folk roots and towards the more introspective soul-searching of his later work.

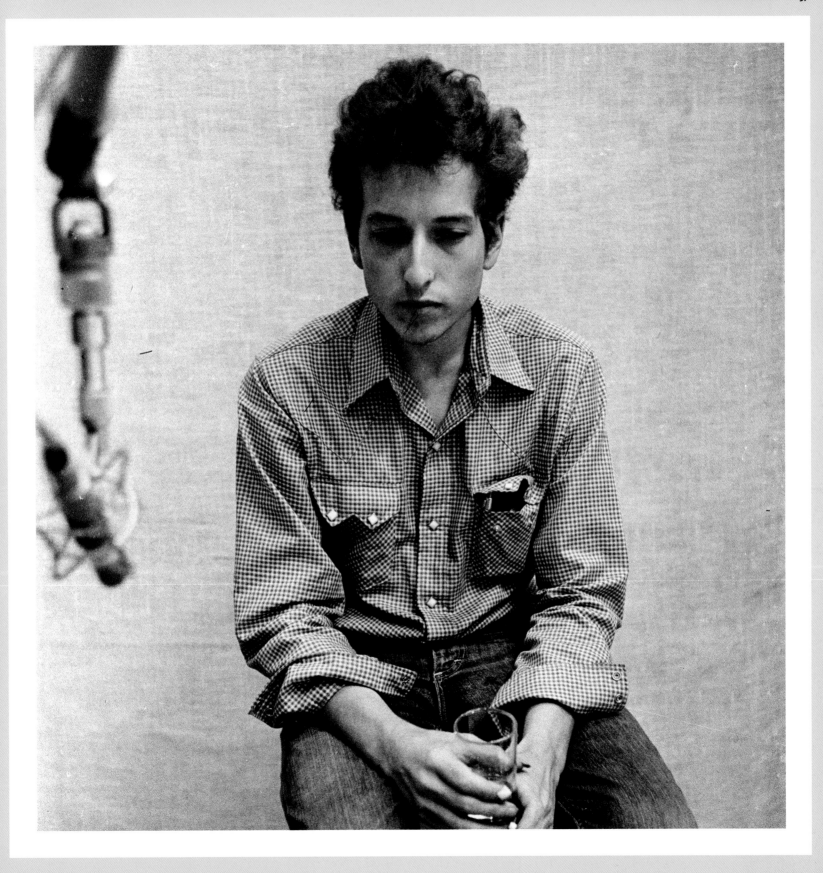

Folk icon

Opposite: Although Dylan, in his own mind, was by now musically probably far from where his folk audience wanted him to be, he continued to perform solo acoustic sets that generally satisfied the folk crowd. In August 1964 Dylan met The Beatles on one of their early US tours, apparently introducing them to cannabis in a New York hotel room. John Lennon, in particular, was influenced by Dylan's music and lyrics. Dylan and George Harrison would become friends and, later, fellow band members in the Traveling Wilburys.

Right: The 1964 Newport Folk Festival saw Dylan once again the centre of attention. The event also brought Dylan together for the first time with the singer Johnny Cash, who was to be a friend in later years and on whose TV show Dylan later guested.

Bringing It All Back Home

Opposite: In January 1965 Dylan began the recording sessions for the ground-breaking *Bringing It All Back Home* album, the first of three records that in eighteen months were to change the face of popular music. Released in March of that year, one side of the album was acoustic and so at least apparently close to Dylan's earlier sound, but with tracks such as "Mr Tambourine Man" marking a move to stranger, denser and apparently drugs-influenced lyrics.

Above: Dylan and friends in Los Angeles in 1965.

Cover artists

Above: Dylan with Sonny and Cher, one of pop music's golden couples of the mid 1960s and who had a hit with the Dylan song "All I Really Want To Do". All through his career Dylan's songs have been performed successfully by others, from the Byrds' huge hit with "Mr Tambourine Man", Jimi Hendrix redefining "All Along The Watchtower", to Gabrielle's number one hit "Rise" which cleverly samples Dylan's "Knockin' On Heaven's Door".

Opposite: Dylan looking stressed. The 1965–66 trilogy of great albums and the tours accompanying them were also notable for Dylan's apparent discovery of both mind-expanding and fatigue-denying substances. If this is the case, they both influenced his song-writing profoundly and kept him on his feet through a maelstrom of touring before audiences many of whom were ambivalent at best about Dylan's new sound.

Don't Look Back

Opposite and right: Between April and June 1965 Dylan toured the UK. Concert performances, along with behind the scenes footage of Dylan and his entourage, were filmed by D. A. Pennebaker for what became one of the most famous rock documentaries of all time, *Don't Look Back*. In the documentary Dylan is shown still performing acoustic sets (though by now he had already recorded with a backing band) and dealing with the pressures of fame and obsessive interest from both fans and journalists.

Centre of attention

Left: Savoy Hotel, London, 1965. Pennebaker filmed the charismatic Dylan mixing with UK celebrities whom came to pay him court, including an over-awed Donovan and a drunken Alan Price from the Animals. The Beatles also visited Dylan, but – probably wisely – declined to be filmed by Pennebaker during their visits.

Opposite: Dylan and Baez during the UK tour. Baez probably thought that Dylan would invite her to perform with him in England in front of an audience that knew Dylan better than it did Baez, returning the favour she had been doing for him in the US. She was to be disappointed and, worse, Dylan appeared to be tired of her company. Baez eventually walked out of Dylan's tour, the film and, for some years, his life.

Hip Young American

Opposite and left: Dylan came across well in *Don't Look Back*, which was eventually released in 1967 at a time when audiences were hungry for any sight of the by then reclusive star. Although there were snippets of performance material, most of Pennebaker's film centred on Dylan and his entourage, as well as the interaction of the hip young Americans and their often bemused British hosts.

Last solo tour

Opposite: Although he covered it well in performance, it must have irritated Dylan to perform solo with guitar and harmonica, when his first electric songs were already in the public domain. "Subterranean Homesick Blues" with its famous video featuring Dylan behind the Savoy Hotel in London, holding cue cards with the lyrics to the song before casting each aside, was filmed on this tour and was inserted by Pennebaker at the beginning of the film.

Above: Dylan, with flower, looking inscrutable. When asked in Pennebaker's film by young English fans why he'd recorded with a band, Dylan joked "I have to give some work to my friends," but this was to be his last solo tour and his "friends" were to feature far more prominently in his music in the months to come.

Hanging out in Woodstock

Opposite: Dylan (with John Sebastian of the Lovin' Spoonful on pillion) rides a motorbike in Woodstock. Dylan came to spend more and more time in and around Woodstock, first at manager Albert Grossman's home, later in his own properties. A motorcycle accident was later to change the course of Dylan's life.

Right: Dylan with poet Allen Ginsberg. Ginsberg was for Dylan a link to Kerouac and the Beat writers who had influenced his earlier reading. Dylan fascinated the poet, who was attracted to both the man and his music.

Writer at work

Opposite: The artist at the typewriter. Dylan found songwriting easy and natural throughout the early part of his career. It was only in the late 1980s that he began to find the songs drying up, before a return to form in the late 1990s.

Above: Dylan pictured with the writer Terry Southern and John Sebastian in the cafe at Woodstock in 1964.

Like A Rolling Stone

Opposite and above: Shortly after returning from the UK tour Dylan began work on the songs that would be included in his next album. In June he was in the studio, once again with Tom Wilson – and this time with a band – working on "Like A Rolling Stone" which went through numerous studio takes before becoming the song finally released as a single in the summer of 1965 and which became one of Dylan's biggest-ever top 40 hits.

"Like A Rolling Stone" is for some Dylan's greatest song and the snare drumbeat that kicks it off one of the best-known moments in rock music. Dylan had probably written the lyrics just after his return from the *Don't Look Back* tour of the UK in the form of what he called "a long piece of vomit" in prose-poem form.

In the studio

Opposite: Dylan in the studio with Mike Bloomfield. Bloomfield, one of the great white blues guitarists, received a phone call out of the blue to ask if he would play on the sessions at which "Like A Rolling Stone" was recorded. He was to have intermittent contact with Dylan in the years to come but this was perhaps his most significant contribution to Bob's music.

Right: Unlike many Dylan recordings, where the first or second take is the one that ends up on the album, Dylan was unusually thoughtful – or even indecisive – about this song and went through more than a dozen different versions of what was to become "Like A Rolling Stone", some of them radically different in tempo and style from the finally released version.

Goodbye to Tom Wilson

Above: Dylan listening to playbacks in the studio control room with manager Albert Grossman (centre) and producer Tom Wilson (second left). Wilson and Dylan were to fall out after this session, with the result Wilson did not work with Dylan again and was replaced by Bob Johnston for the remainder of the *Highway 61* sessions.

Opposite: Although best known for playing an acoustic guitar and harmonica, Dylan is also a distinctive keyboard player, contributing beautiful piano parts to some of the *Highway 61* tracks. These days in concert, Dylan is more likely to be seen playing keyboards than strapping on a guitar and taking centre-stage.

Going electric at Newport

Opposite: In July 1965, in the midst of the sessions for what was to become the *Highway 61 Revisited* album, Dylan once again played the Newport Folk Festival, starting out with an acoustic set (and seen here with the young Donovan, bottom right, on the acoustic stage at Newport) that pleased the folk crowd.

Above: When Dylan came back to the Newport stage later, this time with an electric backing band, and launched into loud and raucous rock 'n' roll, a profound change was signalled: some of the audience clapped; many booed. Dylan seemed taken aback by the response and came back to perform an acoustic version of "It's All Over Now, Baby Blue" which seemed at the same time both to appease the folkies and say goodbye to his old audience, which in retrospect was exactly what the Newport appearance signalled.

Highway 61 Revisited

Opposite and right: Although perhaps a little shaken by his Newport experience, Dylan was soon back in the studio recording more tracks for *Highway 61 Revisited*. This, the second of the great mid-sixties trilogy, was from start to end a powerful rock album, fusing Dylan's increasingly introspective and poetic lyrics with catchy tunes, virtuoso playing and a rock beat. The *Highway 61* tracks include Dylan classic songs such as "Desolation Row", "Just Like Tom Thumb's Blues" and "Ballad Of A Thin Man".

Positively Fourth Street

Opposite and left: At the *Highway 61* sessions Dylan and the band also completed two songs not included on the album, but released as singles: "Can You Please Crawl Out Your Window" and "Positively Fourth Street", a song widely believed to be Dylan's retort to the New York folk crowd who begrudged his move towards the rock mainstream and who accused him of "selling out" at Newport.

Talking to the press

Opposite and left: Dylan faces the press in Los Angeles, September 1965. After finishing *Highway 61 Revisited* (which was released in August) Dylan decided to take his new sound on the road, hiring a backing band and playing a number of stadium shows across the US. He quickly became used to being booed by fans who wanted the acoustic folk artist, rather than the new rock style.

Dylan persevered with the new music, giving press interviews that cemented his status as a funny, witty, and unfathomable hero to much of a generation who treated with usually good-humoured contempt the inane questions he often faced. His lyrics, sound, and attitude were winning him new fans by the thousand.

Famous friends

Left and opposite: Dylan with Brian Jones of the Rolling Stones in New York, November 1965. Dylan was surrounded by a sycophantic crowd and hung out with many famous friends, including the Stones, having quickly left the folk scene far behind. He was also on the fringes of Andy Warhol's artistic milieu and the New York Factory scene.

Although out and about in New York, Dylan was about to become a married man, secretly tying the knot with ex-Bunny Girl Sara Lownds in late November 1965. The beautiful, inscrutable Sara was the inspiration for some of his best-known songs ("Sara" and "Sad Eyed Lady Of The Lowlands"). Bob and Sara moved out to the bohemian setting of Woodstock in upstate New York and began to raise a family, whilst on stage and in the press, Dylan remained in a maelstrom of publicity, adulation and the anger of his former fans.

Touring

Left: Dylan on stage in Berkeley, California, December 1965. The tour continued, as did the media frenzy. Dylan was, by this time, being backed by the Hawks, formerly backing band to singer Ronnie Hawkins, but now accomplished musicians in their own right and able to cope better than most have been with Dylan's unpredictable stage presence and demands.

Above: An exhausted-looking Dylan with musicians Al Kooper (left) and Doug Sahm. In the early part of 1966 the punishing tour schedule continued, but Dylan worked in the studio when the schedule allowed, recording songs for what was to be the third great studio album in eighteen months: *Blonde On Blonde*.

Visiting Denmark

Above and opposite: Albert Grossman, with Dylan looking perhaps a little Hamlet-like. In May 1966 the world tour brought Dylan and his entourage to Denmark, which gave Dylan the opportunity to see the castle of Elsinore and film more scenes for what was to become the *Eat The Document* film. The svengali-like Grossman had less to do when Dylan stopped touring and recording and went on to manage other acts,

notably Janis Joplin. Grossman continued to manage Dylan's career for several years, but they eventually fell out, Dylan taking exception to the extent to which his manager shared in royalties and income. They became embroiled in a long-running court battle which had still not been settled when Grossman died suddenly in 1986.

Friends

Above: Richard Manuel of The Band with Dylan in Copenhagen. Manuel co-wrote one of Dylan's most famous songs, "I Shall Be Released" and contributed to the band's brilliant three-part harmony singing with Rick Danko and Levon Helm.

Opposite: Dylan with an apparently shy Howard Alk. A noted film-maker, Alk worked with Dylan on numerous projects, including *Eat The Document* and *Renaldo And Clara*.

Stagecraft

Above: A thoughtful-looking Dylan contemplates his next move onstage at one of the Danish concerts in May 1965 and (opposite) Rick Danko and Robbie Robertson of The Band onstage with Dylan.

Blonde On Blonde

Above: Dylan faces the press in Paris, May 1966. The album completed, the tour continued. Dylan and the Hawks played songs from the new album to audiences around the world, including Dylan classics like "Just Like A Woman", "Visions Of Johanna" and "I Want You" as well as earlier songs reinterpreted in what was, for the mid-sixties, a huge rock sound never before heard and which continued to draw boos and catcalls from audiences which apparently felt obliged to make that response.

Opposite: Dylan would play an acoustic set, usually to rapturous applause. Then, after the interval, the full band would come out and deliver the rock sound some loved, but which baffled and angered others. On 17 May, in a UK concert at the Manchester Free Trade Hall, came the now famous shout of "Judas!" from a disgruntled member of the audience, provoking the equally famous response from Dylan: "I don't BELIEVE you. You're a liar," before he turned to the band with the demand that they "play fucking loud", launching into a coruscating version of "Like A Rolling Stone".

The 1966 Tour

Opposite and right: On 24 May 1966, his twenty-fifth birthday, Dylan played the Olympia in Paris, to the usual mixture of adulation and booing.

The sound of Dylan and the Hawks in Manchester on this momentous world tour is captured in *The Bootleg Series Volume Four: Bob Dylan Live 1966- The "Royal Albert Hall" Concert"* (so called because the Free Trade Hall concert had for many years been supposed to be the one performed a few days later at the Albert Hall and had been famously issued as a bootleg record with that title). Looking back over 40 years later, it may be hard to understand why audiences found this music quite so challenging, but it is easy to hear the power and passion of performances that even now are staggering in their ability to move the listener.

Eat The Document

Above: Dylan with D.A. Pennebaker (top hat and camera) and Mickey Jones (sunglasses). Pennebaker, who had filmed the *Don't Look Back* documentary of Dylan's 1965 UK tour, had been hired again by Dylan to film the 1966 shows, for a film Dylan wanted to make himself and which was later released as the difficult but fascinating *Eat The Document*, although the film has still never had an official release and unofficial copies are prized by collectors. Jones was at this point in the tour the Hawks' drummer.

Opposite: Dylan looks tired and thoughtful. Back in Woodstock in July, during a break from the pressure of touring, Dylan was trying to put together the *Eat The Document* film. He was also under a tight deadline trying to finish the strange prose poem-novel eventually published years later as *Tarantula*. Albert Grossman had scheduled further tour dates and Dylan was feeling pressure from all sides. On 29 July he fell off a motorbike whilst riding in Woodstock. Rumours flew about the seriousness of the injuries Dylan suffered. He went to ground, spent months recuperating and the frenetic life he had led over the previous months had come abruptly to an end.

Family man in Woodstock

Opposite and above: After the motorbike accident Dylan was largely freed from career commitments and settled down to life in the country with Sara, raising his growing family. The five members of the Hawks (soon to find fame in their own right as The Band) also gravitated towards Dylan in Woodstock. Photographer Elliott Landy had rare access to the Dylans at home. These affecting photographs show Bob, Sara and their growing family in images of contentment at odds with the frenetic life Dylan had been leading before the accident.

The Basement Tapes

Opposite and above: Dylan and family. For many months during 1967 Dylan and The Band came together almost daily in the basement of a house called Big Pink and made the music that came to be known (and famously bootlegged) as The Basement Tapes. These strange, wonderful recordings, most of which remain unreleased officially, show Dylan and the Band improvising and having fun, recording new Dylan originals, alongside folk songs and pop standards, in a relaxed mood far from the high octane noise they had been making on the road only a year before.

Tribute to Woody

Above: Woody Guthrie finally succumbed to Huntington's Chorea in 1967. In January 1968 Dylan made a rare public appearance (his first since the motorbike accident) at a tribute evening for the man whose music had so influenced his early career. Backed by The Band, Dylan joined Pete Seeger, Tom Paxton and other folk luminaries to perform rousing versions of Guthrie songs.

Opposite: The members of The Band, Richard Manuel, Rick Danko, Robbie Robertson, Garth Hudson and Levon Helm, with Ed Sullivan in 1969. Although famous for backing Dylan, The Band made magnificent music in their own right. Their first album, *Music From Big Pink*, released in 1968, mixed folk and country, blues and soul sounds to great effect. Their second album, called simply *The Band*, followed a year later and is felt by many to be both their finest recording and one of the best rock albums of all time.

John Wesley Harding

Opposite and left: Dylan at home in Woodstock. At the end of 1967 he released a new album, *John Wesley Harding*, recorded in Nashville. In its quiet, introspective style, strange characters and biblical imagery it had something in common with The Basement Tapes music, but little with Dylan's last three rock albums. This was a world away from the psychedelia of the Beatles' *Sergeant Pepper* and the Rolling Stones' *Their Satanic Majesties Request* released at around the same time.

Part Two

Back on the Road

Stepping out

Left: Dylan and wife Sara. In Woodstock the Dylans found contentment in family life and in Bob's music with The Band.

Opposite: *John Wesley Harding* further cemented Dylan in the eyes of fans as an enigmatic genius who did not choose to follow the musical crowd. One of the songs from the album, "All Along The Watchtower", would be covered brilliantly by Jimi Hendrix and was to become one of Dylan's best-known songs, often played by him in concert in later years.

An appearance with Johnny Cash

Opposite and above: Dylan appeared on Johnny Cash's TV show in 1969, a rare public appearance by Dylan after years of reclusive seclusion in Woodstock. Although reportedly terrified at the prospect of singing on national TV, Dylan delivered fine performances, including his duet with Cash on "Girl From The North Country". A version of this song was included on the *Nashville Skyline* album.

Nashville Skyline

Opposite: Dylan's next album, *Nashville Skyline*, released in 1969, was yet another change of direction: a country-rock album sung by Dylan in a new voice: a soft sweet tenor far from any he had previously used. The album contained the classic track "Lay Lady Lay".

Right: Dylan in the studio at the *Nashville Skyline* recording sessions. Johnny Cash joined Dylan in the studio and the two recorded a number of tracks together.

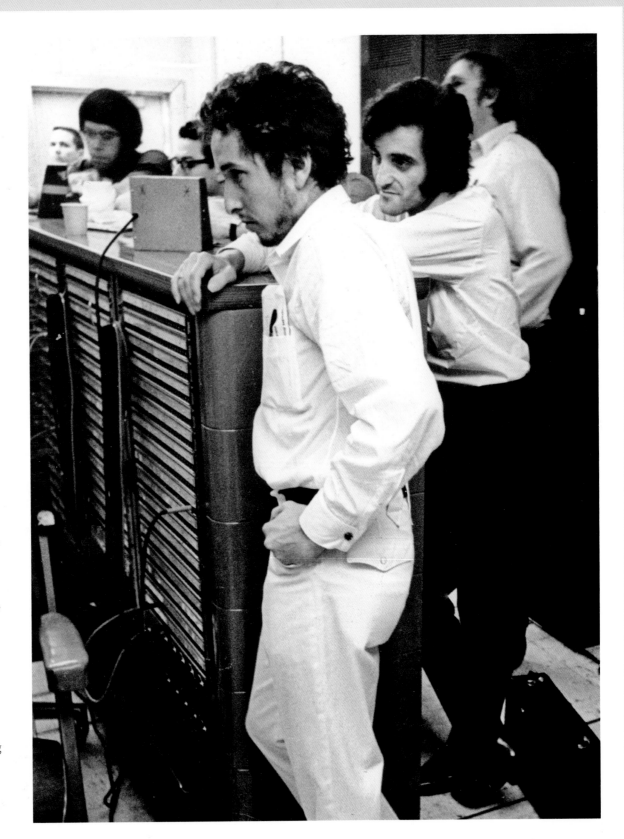

Isle of Wight Festival

Opposite and above: Dylan was tempted out of Woodstock seclusion to perform at the August 1969 Isle of Wight festival in Britain, his first major live performance for three years and an eagerly awaited appearance by a man whose reputation as genius and spokesman for a generation had only grown during the low-profile years. Dylan chose to play the Isle of Wight rather than feature at the landmark Woodstock Festival which took place in the same month in upstate New York (although actually 60 miles away from the town itself). A white-suited Dylan closed the festival, backed by The Band in a low-key set that lasted barely an hour and disappointed many festival-goers.

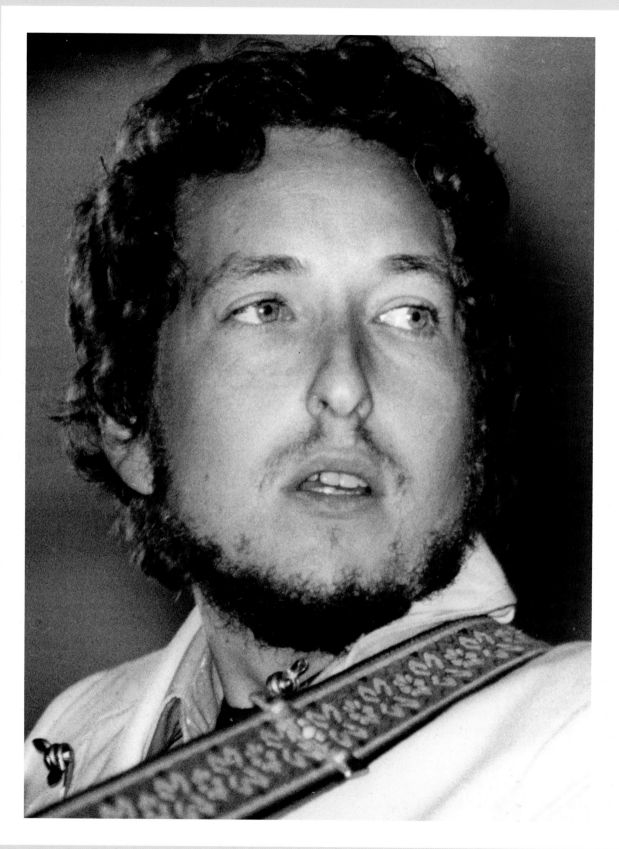

Moving on

Opposite and left: Dylan on stage at the Isle of Wight festival. Woodstock was attracting more and more visitors keen to find the Dylan house and meet their hero. The family eventually grew tired of this and after returning from Europe the Dylans moved to New York to live in Greenwich Village, where the younger Dylan had first found fame. Here he began slowly to emerge from the seclusion of the Woodstock years. 1970's *Self Portrait* album baffled and disappointed many fans, with its cover versions and small evidence of Dylan's songwriting genius. The follow-up *New Morning* pleased fans more, with Dylan writing original material and sounding more like his old self.

The Concert for Bangladesh

Opposite: Dylan and George Harrison at the Concert for Bangladesh. Of all the Beatles, George Harrison was the one to whom Dylan became closest. When Harrison organized a charity concert in August 1971 in support of the flood-hit people of Bangladesh he invited Dylan to play. The concert was the Live Aid of its day, the first time such a group of musical star talent had gathered to play in a good cause.

Above: Dylan and Leon Russell at the Concert for Bangladesh. Dylan wore denim and, with acoustic guitar and harmonica, looked quite unlike the white-suited Isle of Wight performer and more like the Dylan of old. Playing classic songs such as "Blowin' In The Wind" and "A Hard Rain's a-Gonna Fall", Dylan's was the star appearance in a stellar line-up.

Returning to his roots

Above and opposite: George Harrison, Dylan and Leon Russell at the Bangladesh concert in Madison Square Garden, New York. The film of the concert, and the sound-track album released later that year, served to enhance Dylan's reputation as having "come back" from the years of seclusion. Dylan was more visible, recording with the poet Allen Ginsberg, releasing a further greatest hits album and making music with various friends and acquaintances from the rock world. An old-fashioned but topical protest song, "George Jackson", released in November 1971, further reinforced the sense of Dylan having returned to his roots and on New Year's Eve 1971 Dylan appeared as a special guest at a concert by The Band, a live recording of which was released as the album *Rock Of Ages*.

A man called Alias

Opposite: In November 1972 Dylan and his family arrived in Durango, Mexico, where Dylan was to film a role in the Sam Peckinpah film *Pat Garrett and Billy the Kid*. Dylan was fulfilling a long-held desire to work in mainstream cinema and he had already agreed to provide sound-track music for the film. His character was called Alias, not one of the leading roles, but, because of Dylan's reputation and charisma, a striking performance.

Above: Dylan with Kris Kristofferson (who played Billy the Kid in the film) on the set. In the early part of 1973, in between shooting, Dylan recorded the film's sound-track in California. The music Dylan and his band produced was just right in feel for the film Peckinpah was making. One track in particular, "Knockin' On Heaven's Door", was perfect for a scene where a dying Slim Pickens is comforted by Katy Jurado and the song became a major and well-loved hit for Dylan.

Pat Garrett

Left: Alias and horse on the *Pat Garrett* set. Sam Peckinpah was a famous director with films such as *The Wild Bunch* and *Straw Dogs* to his credit. He was impressed with the music Dylan had written for the film, but their working relationship deteriorated as Peckinpah seemed to become jealous of the attention Dylan attracted on set. Tales abound of Peckinpah's eccentricity during filming.

Opposite: The *Pat Garrett* sound-track album was released in July 1973, by which time Dylan and family had relocated from New York to California. Dylan now began to discuss a "comeback" tour and album with The Band, as well as striking a record deal with David Geffen's Asylum Records, leaving Columbia for the first time in his recording career. In November, Dylan and The Band recorded *Planet Waves* in Los Angeles, their only studio album together, Dylan's first proper studio album in three years and the one containing one of his most popular songs, "Forever Young".

Moving west

Right: Dylan photographed at the Palomino Club in Los Angeles and (opposite) in an audience in 1973. Although they already had homes in Arizona, The Hamptons and New York, the Dylans decided to settle on the Point Dume peninsula, a few miles north of Malibu Beach, in 1973.

Tour '74

Left: Commencing on 3 January, Tour '74, as it came to be known, marked the first time a major artist had embarked on a multi-city stadium tour on such a scale. Demand for tickets was huge and press and audience expectations ran high. Dylan and his colleagues did not disappoint.

Opposite: From left: Rick Danko, Levon Helm and Robbie Robertson of The Band on stage with Dylan during Tour '74. By the time the tour closed on 14 February, Dylan and The Band had played 65 shows, getting a hero's welcome everywhere, in stark contrast to the famous shows barely eight years previously when they had been booed for playing similar music. Although he later claimed not to have enjoyed the experience of touring and the music was by no means subtle, Dylan's vocals were assured and the shows confirmed his status as a powerful and charismatic live performer.

Before The Flood

Opposite: A live album from the '74 tour was released by Asylum that June, Dylan's second and last album for Geffen's label. After this, he returned to Columbia, where he has stayed ever since. The cover of *Before The Flood* carried an image of fans lighting matches and holding lighters in a darkened auditorium as an act of homage to Dylan, behaviour typical of modern concert-goers, but a practice established on this tour.

Above: The live album was ironically titled, in that after years of stability the certainties of Dylan's stable family life were about to be washed away. Rumours about the state of his marriage had circulated for some time, but by the summer it was being reported publicly that Bob and Sara were splitting up. Although this was not the end (the relationship would continue in an on–off fashion for several years), it was certainly the end of the life of the quiet family man.

Friends of Chile

Above: The Friends of Chile benefit concert, May 1974: Dylan with Dave Van Ronk (right) and other assorted folk singers at the charity event organized by Dylan's old folk buddy Phil Ochs. Dylan was visibly the worse for wear at this concert, he and Ochs having reputedly drunk a significant amount of cheap red wine together before going on stage.

Performing with Arlo Guthrie

Above: Arlo Guthrie and Dylan onstage at the Friends of Chile benefit with Dave Van Ronk (far right). Dylan and Guthrie had first met in 1961 in New York when Dylan visited the Guthrie household unannounced, looking for Arlo's father Woody, Dylan's early idol. Woody was by that time in hospital, but Arlo remembered the meeting with the aspiring folk singer. Performing with his hero's son would have been a poignant moment for Dylan.

Opposite: Dylan spent the spring and summer of 1975 socializing, attending concerts, playing the occasional guest appearance himself. Meanwhile, the songs for a new album were coming together and the idea for another tour was forming, but this time a tour a world away from the bombast of Tour '74.

SNACK

Opposite and above: In March 1975 Dylan was persuaded by concert promoter Bill Graham to appear at his SNACK (Students Need Athletics, Culture and Kicks) charity concert at Kezar Stadium, Golden Gate Park, in San Francisco. Dylan was joined by Neil Young along with Ben Keith and Tim Drummond as well as members of The Band at the event.

Blood On The Tracks

Opposite and above: Dylan and friends pictured on stage performing at the SNACK benefit. Sara can be glimpsed sitting at the side of the stage (above). The Dylans' marriage, although shaky, was not yet over.

Through the summer and fall of 1974 Dylan was composing the songs for what many consider his finest album, *Blood On The Tracks*. Recording most of the album in New York in September, Dylan took the acetates with him when spending Christmas with his family in Minnesota. On his brother David's recommendation he decided to change the feel of some tracks, hired local musicians and, in a Minneapolis recording studio, re-recorded part of the album over the holidays. Released in January 1975, *Blood On The Tracks* appears to address the disintegration of a marriage and has been heard by fans (to Dylan's irritation) as a chronicle of the break-up of his marriage with Sara.

Desire

Opposite and right: On stage in San Francisco. Dylan spent most of the summer of 1975 in New York, apart from Sara, writing the songs for the *Desire* album, many of which were co-written with theatrical producer Jacques Levy. The album was recorded in the autumn, with Emmylou Harris's backing vocals and Scarlet Rivera's violin making for one of the most distinctive and cohesive sounds of Dylan's recording career and a more than respectable follow-up to the remarkable *Blood On The Tracks*. One of the tracks, "Hurricane", was as gripping a protest song as Dylan had ever written, about Rubin "Hurricane" Carter, a black boxer wrongly convicted of a triple murder.

Rolling Thunder

Opposite and above: Joni Mitchell, Richie Havens, Joan Baez, Ramblin' Jack Elliot, Dylan and T-Bone Burnette on stage. In the autumn of 1975 Dylan went out on the road again, but this time on a tour deliberately much smaller in scale than Tour '74. Accompanied by Baez, Allen Ginsberg and many other artists and friends from his early folk days, the gloriously ramshackle Rolling Thunder Revue toured small venues and allowed Dylan to sing and play with a passion and vitality rarely seen even by his audiences. The tour concluded in December at Madison Square Garden with the "night of the Hurricane" where Dylan and Muhammad Ali led an all-star fund-raising evening for the boxer's release campaign.

Farewell concert

Opposite: On 25 November 1976 Dylan appeared at The Band's star-studded farewell concert, filmed by Martin Scorsese as *The Last Waltz*. Here they are pictured arriving at the Winterland Ballroom in San Francisco, the venue for the show, for a sound check.

Above: Dylan with Robbie Robertson on stage at the Winterland Ballroom.

The Last Waltz

Above: Having decided to cease touring and recording, Dylan's old backing band went out on a high note, with numerous special guests, including Joni Mitchell, Neil Diamond, Neil Young and their old band leader Ronnie Hawkins appearing during the evening to perform with The Band.

Opposite: From left: Neil Diamond, Doctor John, Joni Mitchell, Neil Young, Rick Danko, Dylan and Robbie Robertson on the Winterland stage. The stage furnishings had been borrowed from a local production of the opera *La Traviata* and formed an incongruous, though sumptuous, backdrop to the parade of '6os counter-culture heroes on stage.

I Shall Be Released

Opposite and above: Van Morrison, Dylan and The Band's guitarist and principal songwriter, Robbie Robertson, perform at The Last Waltz. Dylan and The Band performed some of their 1966 tour songs, along with material from *Planet Waves,* before the concert's finale where the whole cast sang Dylan's "I Shall Be Released". Dylan and the legendary Morrison have performed together on several occasions over the years, including a joint tour in 1998.

End of a marriage

Above: Bob driving Sara in 1976. The Dylans' marriage had been on the rocks for some time. In spite of the heartfelt plea in the song "Sara" on *Desire*, which seemed to have brought about a partial reconciliation for a time, Sara filed for divorce in March 1977.

Opposite: While divorce and custody battles over the children continued, Dylan was putting together a film from scenes shot during the first Rolling Thunder tour. Released in January 1978, *Renaldo and Clara* is a baffling film, even for dedicated fans, although if one can sit through its four and a half hours of strangeness, there are some great concert scenes from the Rolling Thunder Revue.

Planning a tour

Opposite and right: In 1978 Dylan was planning a world tour, the first time he would tour extensively outside the US in many years. He recruited a large backing band and rehearsed numerous songs from his by now huge back catalogue.

Escaping the critics

Opposite and left: At the beginning of 1978 Dylan's monumental four-hour film *Renaldo and Clara* was released to almost universally scathing reviews. He was able to escape some of the criticism when the world tour began in Japan on 20 February, Dylan's first ever concert in the country. Dylan's presence evoked huge interest among Japanese fans. Some of the shows there were recorded and a selection of the tracks later released as the live album *Bob Dylan at Budokan*.

Street-Legal

Opposite and left: Dylan on stage in 1978. The tour continued, Dylan arriving in London in June to deliver six highly acclaimed shows at Earls Court. This month also saw the release of *Street-Legal*, an intriguing album that divides fans and critics, but contains strong songs such as "Senor (Tales Of Yankee Power)" and Dylan's last (fairly) big hit single "Baby Stop Crying".

A low ebb

Opposite and right: The American leg of Dylan's world tour was generally less positively received than it had been in other territories. The big band sound and the reworking of many greatest hits in unfamiliar styles was not to the taste of some audiences. By December 1978, as the tour drew to a close, Dylan was at a low ebb. The American shows had been poorly received; *Renaldo and Clara* was still being derided; his personal life was, by his own admission, in a mess.

Born again

Opposite and above: On 24 November, in Fort Worth, Texas, Dylan wore round his neck a crucifix thrown onto the stage by a fan at an earlier concert. Soon afterwards he began to perform songs with overtly religious content. In January 1979, shortly after the tour ended, Dylan was "born again" and in April recorded the first of his religious albums, *Slow Train Coming*. Once again he confounded his fans, many of whom were outraged that Dylan, the man who had once told them not to follow leaders, was now literally preaching at them about the need to follow Jesus.

Gospel tour

Opposite and above: With a new band and gospel backing singers, Dylan toured the US through the autumn of 1979 and continued into 1980. He would stop the music to preach at bemused and sometimes angry audiences. His earlier music was almost entirely absent from the gospel shows, which added to the irritation of these events for many fans.

Gotta Serve Somebody

Above: An unusually smart-looking Dylan at the Grammy Awards ceremony in February 1980, where he won the award for "best male rock vocal performance" in 1979 for "Gotta Serve Somebody" from *Slow Train Coming*, which was – albeit grudgingly by many- generally reckoned a powerful album.

The preaching stops

Opposite and above: At the after-show party at the Grammies, a once-again scruffy Dylan talks to Rickie Lee Jones. Dylan continued to write, record and perform religious songs during the early 1980s, but *Saved* was a disappointing follow-up album to its predecessor and *Shot Of Love* in 1981 began the reintroduction of non-religious material in Dylan's writing. In his concerts Dylan also began to include older material, to the relief of some fans.

Infidels and touring

Opposite and right: Dylan and Joan Baez in Hamburg in 1984. Dylan released *Infidels* in November 1983. Typical of Dylan's middle and later periods, great tracks recorded in the studio are left off the album (in this case including the Dylan classic "Blind Willie McTell") and inferior tracks released, making the whole a curate's egg of a record. In spring 1984 Dylan took his new songs on the road in Europe, with a new band and with Joan Baez and Carlos Santana performing on the same bill. Baez and Dylan fell out soon and this would be the last time the two would share a stage.

Live Aid

Opposite and above: In January 1985 Dylan participated in the recording of the star-studded "We Are The World" charity single. On 13 July, Dylan was given the honour of being the closing act at Bob Geldof's Live Aid concert in Philadelphia. Backed by Rolling Stones Keith Richards and Ronnie Wood, what should have been a triumph was a disaster: the three gave a shambolic performance as Dylan delivered lacklustre versions of classic songs, appeared nervous and spoiled the moment by asking whether some of the donations destined for Africa could be redirected to American farmers.

Dylan on stage with the Heartbreakers at Farm Aid

Opposite: For Dylan, two good things came out of Live Aid. First, Dylan's comments there about poor farmers encouraged Willie Nelson and others to put together a charity event on their behalf at which Dylan was invited to appear. Second, Dylan was backed at the event by Tom Petty and the Heartbreakers, who were to prove an able backing band for several years and who, at Farm Aid, helped Dylan deliver a sharp performance that somewhat redeemed the Live Aid debacle.

Above: Dylan on stage with Tom Petty and the Heartbreakers. On the left of this photograph is Carolyn Dennis, one of Dylan's backing singers at the time and, between 1986 and 1992, his wife. Dylan's second marriage was a closely kept secret that became generally known only with the publication of a 2001 Dylan biography. The couple had a child, Desiree, and Dylan has been described as a "wonderful, active father" by his ex-wife.

Biograph

Opposite and above: 1985 had been a mixed year for Dylan. A new album, *Empire Burlesque*, had once again received mixed reviews. In October, however, CBS released a boxed set of Dylan material called *Biograph*, mixing classic hits with bootlegs and rare material new even to collectors, along with booklets containing photographs and interviews with Dylan, in what was to become a template for retrospective boxed sets of major artists' material. A tribute evening to Dylan at the launch of *Biograph* was attended by David Bowie (pictured here), Neil Young and a host of other stars.

True Confessions

Opposite and right: In 1986 Dylan, Petty and the Heartbreakers embarked on what became known as the True Confessions tour, beginning in New Zealand and taking in Australia and Japan, where Dylan played to some of his most loyal and appreciative audiences. Here Dylan and Tom Petty are pictured at Westwood One studios in Los Angeles.

US dates

Opposite and above: Dylan with Tom Petty and the Heartbreakers on stage in San Francisco. The True Confessions Tour eventually arrived in the US and on 9 June 1986 Dylan began an American tour for the first time in five years, at the Sports Arena in San Diego. The tour, which was reasonably well received by audiences, concluded in August, by which time Dylan was almost ready to embark on a new challenge.

Sharing the stage

Above: Dylan with Bono and U2 perform songs from the album *The Joshua Tree* during a concert at Inglewood, California, in 1987 and (opposite) on stage in San Francisco during the True Confessions tour.

Hearts of Fire

Opposite and left: In the autumn of 1986 Dylan filmed *Hearts of Fire*, directed by Richard Marquand and also starring Rupert Everett and Fiona Flanagan (left). The movie was not well received, Dylan's performance being one of the less embarrassing aspects of the film. The venture seemed symptomatic of Dylan's inability to judge, as he had once seemed uniquely able to do, the right project to embark on, the right songs to record and the right career moves to make. Dylan seemed lost and adrift for much of the 1980s.

Dylan and the Dead

Opposite and above: Bob Dylan and The Grateful Dead perform at Oakland County Stadium, San Francisco, on 24 July 1987. He had previously appeared as a guest at concerts by the legendary rock band and in 1987 they embarked on a concert tour together. Although Dylan's music had long inspired members of the band, the consensus was that there was little in their collaboration that inspired audiences. A live album taken from performances on this tour, *Dylan And The Dead*, is generally agreed to be one of Dylan's worst ever official recordings. In 1989, in a bizarre coda to his relationship with the Dead, Dylan actually asked to join the band – a request refused after a vote by band members.

Collaborating

Opposite: Dylan's relationship with George Harrison was partly the cause of the formation of an unlikely supergroup. At Dylan's home studio in Malibu, Harrison brought together the legendary Roy Orbison, Jeff Lynne from ELO and Dylan's recent collaborator Tom Petty to write and record a B-side for his forthcoming single. The five worked well together and decided to make an album which, released under the jokey band name of the Traveling Wilburys, became one of the most successful of the decade. Orbison died not long afterwards and, although the four surviving members made a second album, the magic was gone and a promised tour never materialized.

Above: Dylan on stage with The Grateful Dead in San Francisco, 1987.

Part Three

Reinvented

Bob and The Boss

Opposite and right: Bruce Springsteen, a long-time fan, inducted Dylan into the Rock 'n' Roll Hall of Fame in January 1988. "Elvis freed our bodies and Dylan freed our minds" was Springsteen's pithy summary of the effect those two icons of popular music had had on his generation. It was in 1988 that Dylan embarked on the seemingly incessant round of touring that has continued to the present day, becoming known as the Never Ending Tour.

Legends of popular music

Opposite: Dylan at a tribute concert for the late Roy Orbison, Los Angeles, February 1990. In 1991 *The Bootleg Series Volumes I–III* was released, the first of an ongoing series of albums, the product of delving into the vaults to find rare and previously unreleased material. Dylan's out-takes are better than many artists' main catalogues and the series has contributed to the revival of his reputation since the somewhat lost decade of the 1980s.

Above: Three musical legends: Chuck Berry, Dylan and James Brown.

Thirty years in the business

Above: George Harrison with Dylan at CBS's Thirtieth Anniversary Celebration for Dylan held at Madison Square Garden, New York, in October 1992. A host of celebrities, including Eric Clapton, Neil Young and surviving members of The Band, performed songs from Dylan's back catalogue. Dylan himself finally took the stage, a somewhat awkward centre of attention.

Opposite: In January 1993 Dylan performed at a concert celebrating Bill Clinton's inauguration as President. Although there had been no new album of original material since 1990's poorly received *Under The Red Sky*, Dylan released two albums of traditional folk and blues material in 1992 and 1993 that marked a return to his musical roots and saw him perform alone with only acoustic guitar and harmonica. *Good As I Been To You* and *World Gone Wrong* presented heartfelt and authentic performances, albeit Dylan's voice had now become the old man's growl he had once affected.

Unplugged

Opposite and above: In November 1994 Dylan and his stage band recorded an "Unplugged" concert for MTV. Dylan performed diffidently, but looked cool. He had tried to adapt to the MTV generation during the 1980s, collaborating in a number of videos to accompany songs that should have given, but rarely did, a new generation a reason to enjoy his music. Nevertheless, as the decade progressed Dylan's tarnished reputation began slowly to be restored.

Rubbing shoulders with the famous

Above: Charlton Heston, Lauren Bacall and Bob Dylan receive Kennedy Center lifetime awards from President Clinton in December 1997.

Opposite: The once born-again Dylan performed before Pope John Paul II at a Roman Catholic youth festival in Bologna, Italy, in September. The Pope quoted from "Blowin' in the Wind" in his speech following the performance, describing Christ as "the road a man must walk down before they call him a man".

Time Out Of Mind

Opposite and right: As the decade progressed Bob would eventually lose the writer's block that had dogged him for years: in 1997 he released *Time Out Of Mind*, the first of a trio of albums that have in the past few years rebuilt Dylan's reputation among listeners, critics and the media. At the Grammy Awards in 1998 Dylan received the award for Album of the Year from Sheryl Crow.

Oscar winner

Opposite: Dylan and Madonna at an Academy Awards party in 1999. Dylan himself was to win an Oscar for the song "Things Have Changed", used in the film *Wonder Boys* in 2000. The award seems to have pleased Dylan, as the statuette can usually be seen displayed proudly on stage during his concerts.

Above: Dylan and Eric Clapton perform at the latter's Crossroads charity concert in June 1999. The two have shared a stage many times over the years and Clapton had a hit with his version of "Knockin' On Heaven's Door".

Love And Theft

Above: Dylan on stage, as the Never Ending Tour continues into a new millennium. In 2001 Dylan released *Love And Theft*, another new album of original material. Although initially overshadowed by events, having been released on 9/11, this proved another hugely popular album that cemented the artist's critical renaissance.

Opposite: Singer Ryan Adams, Elton John and Dylan at Elton's AIDS Foundation party in 2002.

Honest With Me

Opposite and above: Dylan performed "Honest With Me" from *Time Out Of Mind* at the 2002 Grammy Awards ceremony. Although other musicians come and go from the tour band, Dylan's bass player Tony Garnier (above, with Dylan) joined the Never Ending Tour band in June 1989 and has remained with his employer longer than any other Dylan band member.

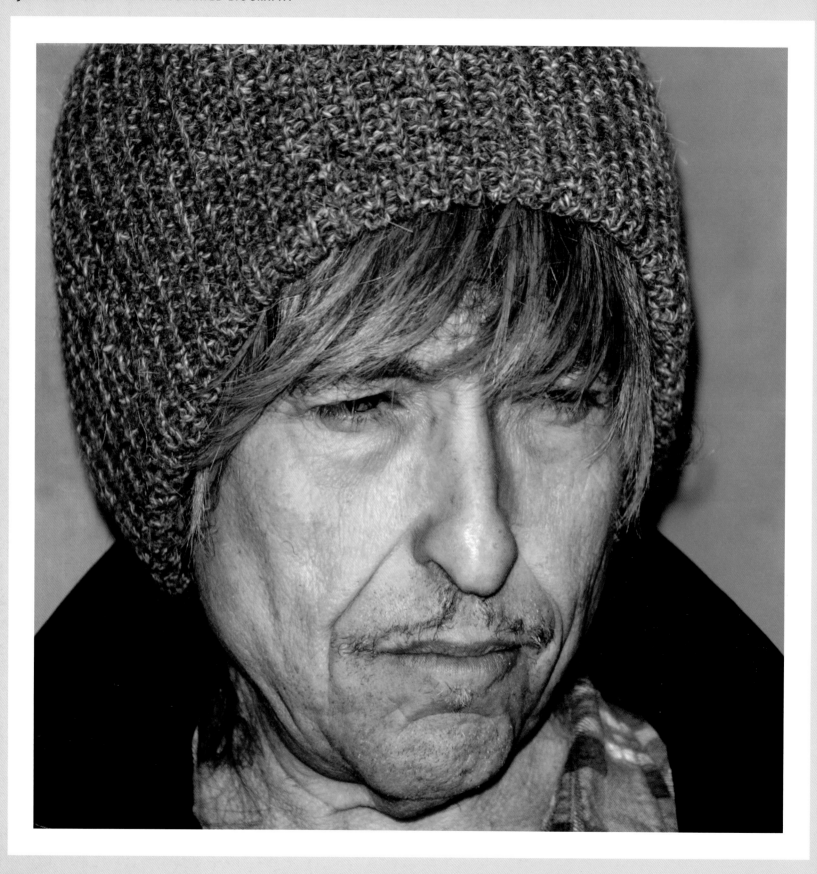

Masked And Anonymous

Opposite and above: Dylan with Jessica Lange at the *Masked And Anonymous* film premiere, Sundance Film Festival, 2003. This was Dylan's first major film role since *Hearts of Fire* and he co-wrote the film with director Larry Charles, albeit under a pseudonym. The story of an iconic rock star released from prison to play a benefit concert, the film was panned by the critics even though it had attracted a host of famous actors keen to work with the legendary musician: John Goodman, Penelope Cruz, Mickey Rourke and Jeff Bridges were just a few of the big names on the list of credits.

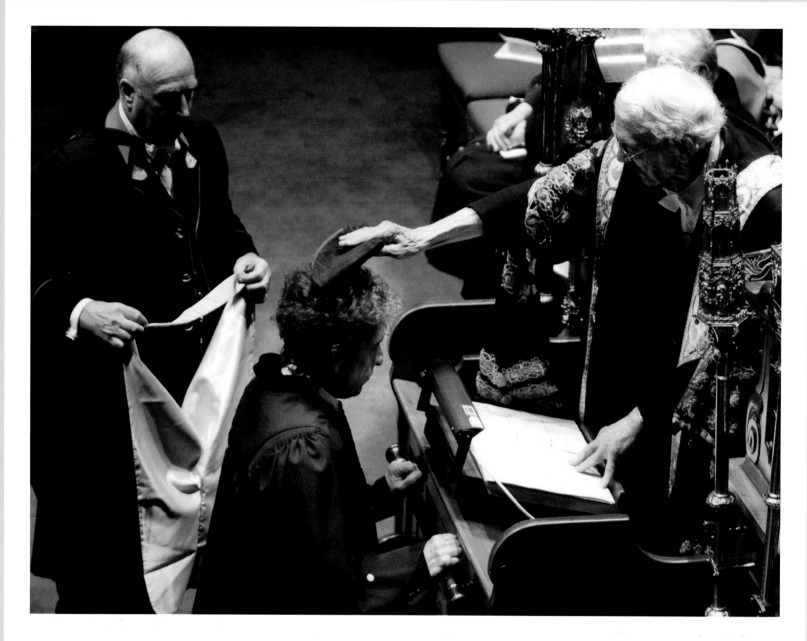

More honours

Above: In June 2004 Dylan received an honorary music degree from the University of St Andrews, Scotland. Strangely, Dylan has a number of connections with Scotland, owning property there and having been a member of the Malt Whisky Society. The narrator in Dylan's acclaimed song "Highlands" from *Time Out Of Mind* even displays a (somewhat shaky) knowledge of and affection for Scottish topography.

Opposite: Dylan makes an appearance in the Willie Nelson and Friends "Outlaws and Angels" show on 5 May 2004.

Chronicles

Above; Bob Dylan performs at The Fleadh at Finsbury Park, London, on 20 June 2004, the London stop of the UK leg of his European tour. In October 2004 the long-awaited book of Dylan's memoirs, *Chronicles Volume I* was published. Perhaps to the surprise of many readers, Dylan reveals himself to be an accomplished and engaging writer, describing his life in early 1960s New York, talking about the Woodstock years and describing in some detail the recording of *Oh Mercy* in 1989. The book was an international best-seller.

Opposite: On stage during Willie Nelson's Outlaws and Angels show at the Wiltern Theater, Los Angeles, on 5 May 2004. During the show, which was later broadcast on television, Willie Nelson and Dylan performed the Hank Williams song "You Win Again".

The Never Ending Tour continues...

Opposite: Dylan at the Apollo Theater, New York. In May 2006, in yet another successful career move that would have been difficult to predict, Dylan became a DJ, with the first broadcast of a weekly radio series, *Theme Time Radio Hour*. Each week Dylan plays songs around a chosen theme, displaying a wide-ranging musical taste, deep knowledge and a sense of humour unsuspected by many. In August of the same year came the release of *Modern Times*, Dylan's third critically lauded album in a row.

Opposite: Dylan performing in New Orleans in 2006. In the song "Tangled Up In Blue" Dylan famously sings that "the only thing I knew how to do was to keep on keepin' on". This is exactly what he seems inclined to do: writing, recording, painting (exhibitions of his "Drawn Blank" series of paintings were a huge success in 2008); and of course the Never Ending Tour continues as Dylan keeps on ...

Chronology
and
Discography

1911

19 October Birth of Dylan's father, Abraham Zimmerman

1915

13 June Birth of Dylan's mother, Beatrice Rutman. Dylan's early Mother's Day rhyme to his mother is probably his first ever surviving writing:

My dear mother, I hope that you
Will never grow old and gray,
So that all the people in the world will say:
'Hello, young lady, Happy Mother's Day'

1934

10 June marriage of Dylan's parents

1941

24 May birth of Robert Allen Zimmerman

1946

February birth of Bob's brother, David Zimmerman

1947

The Zimmerman family moves from Duluth to Hibbing, Minnesota

1954

22 May Bobby Zimmerman's bar mitzvah

1956

Autumn Bobby Zimmerman plays in local band The Shadow Blasters and then forms another band, The Golden Chords. The band continues until 1958

1959

January Bobby Zimmerman sees Buddy Holly play a concert in Duluth, three days before Holly's death in a plane crash. Dylan later speaks of a moment where Holly, apparently, catches his eye and he feels a baton being passed...

June Bob Zimmerman graduates from Hibbing High School

September Bob begins his studies at the University of Minneapolis

October Bob begins to play on the coffeehouse circuit in Minneapolis, gravitating quickly towards the folk music scene there

1960

September Bob reads Woody Guthrie's autobiography, *Bound For Glory*

1961

24 January after moving around the country, playing in folk clubs, Dylan arrives in New York for the first time

25 January Dylan visits Woody Guthrie in Greystone Hospital, New Jersey

13 February Dylan plays Gerde's Folk City for the first time

11 April Dylan's first professional engagement, supporting John Lee Hooker at Gerde's

July Dylan meets Albert Grossman, later to become his manager

October (probably) Dylan plays harmonica on a recording by Harry Belafonte

26 October Dylan signs a recording contract with CBS

20-22 November Dylan records his first album, produced by John Hammond

1962

19 March first LP, *Dylan*, is released

May writes "Blowin' In The Wind"

June now managed by Albert Grossman

9 August changes name officially to Bob Dylan

December visits UK to make the TV play *Madhouse On Castle Street* and plays London folk clubs

1963

12 April first major solo concert at New York Town Hall

12 May walks out of the *Ed Sullivan Show* after intended performance of "Talkin' John Birch Paranoid Blues" is censored

27 May *The Freewheelin' Bob Dylan* is released

26 July first appearance at the Newport Folk Festival

28 August appears at the March on Washington with Joan Baez and others, ahead of Martin Luther King's historic speech

1964

9 June in a single night records the songs for *Another Side Of Bob Dylan*

July appears once again at the Newport Folk Festival

31 October major solo concert at Philharmonic Hall, New York

1965

January begins recording sessions for *Bringing It All Back Home*

April in the UK for the tour that is to be documented in the film *Don't Look Back*

15 June records "Like A Rolling Stone" in New York

25 July goes "electric" at the Newport Folk Festival

3 September Hollywood Bowl concert with The Hawks (later The Band), effectively the start of the world tour

25 November Bob and Sara Lownds are married

1966

February begins recording *Blonde On Blonde* in Nashville

April the world tour reaches Australia

May *Blonde On Blonde* is released

27 May final concert of the world tour at the Royal Albert Hall, London (it was long assumed that this was the scene of the famous "Judas!" shout from the audience recorded on a bootleg of the concert, although the shout and the concert in fact took place at the Manchester Free Trade Hall a few days earlier)

25 July the infamous motorbike accident in Woodstock, after which Dylan withdraws from touring and other commitments

1967

Spring-Autumn for most of the year, Dylan and The Band gather in the basement of the Big Pink house, along with other venues, to record what will become known as The Basement Tapes

October records *John Wesley Harding* in Nashville

1968

20 January appears with The Band at the Woody Guthrie Memorial Concert

5 June Dylan's father Abe dies of a heart attack

1969

February records *Nashville Skyline* in Nashville

31 August plays at the Isle of Wight Festival, UK

1970

June *Self Portrait* is released, the first Dylan record to attract significant negative criticism in the media

September returns from Woodstock to live in Greenwich Village, New York

1971

May *Tarantula* is published. Dylan's long-awaited "novel" is in fact a long prose-poem that baffles most readers

1 August appears at George Harrison's Concert For Bangladesh at Madison Square Garden, New York

November records and releases "George Jackson", a protest song in the old-fashioned mould

1972

Begins filming *Pat Garrett and Billy the Kid* for Sam Peckinpah in Durango, Mexico

1973

February records the sound-track music for *Pat Garrett and Billy the Kid*

November Leaves CBS to sign for David Geffen's Asylum label

November records *Planet Waves* with The Band, their only studio album together

1974

3 January Tour '74 with The Band begins in Chicago

January *Planet Waves* is released

14 February end of the record-breaking Tour '74

9 May plays at the Friends of Chile benefit concert with Phil Ochs and others

September begins recording *Blood On The Tracks* which is to be viewed as one of his greatest achievements

December re-records some of the *Blood On The Tracks* material in Minneapolis, Minnesota

1975

January *Blood On The Tracks* is released

23 March plays at the SNACK benefit concert

June meets Rubin "Hurricane" Carter, on whose behalf he later releases a hit single

July begins recording the songs for *Desire*

October-December The Rolling Thunder Revue tours the US eastern seaboard, Dylan being joined by Joan Baez, Roger McGuinn, Ramblin' Jack Elliott and numerous other artists

8 December Dylan and the Revue join The Night Of The Hurricane all-star charity concert for Rubin Carter at Madison Square Garden

1976

25 January a second Night Of The Hurricane concert in Houston is less successful than the first, actually losing money

April the Rolling Thunder Revue reconvenes for a second tour

23 May the Rolling Thunder show at Fort Collins, Colorado, is filmed and later released as the *Hard Rain* film and live album

25 November performs at The Band's farewell concert, called The Last Waltz, at the Winterland Ballroom in San Francisco

1977

February Bob and Sara Dylan separate

December rehearsals begin for the major world tour scheduled for the following year

1978

January the film *Renaldo and Clara* is released, to critical derision. It nevertheless captures some magnificent live performances from the Rolling Thunder Revue

20 February the 1978 world tour begins in Japan, Dylan is accompanied by a big band and has radically reworked some of his older songs

June *Street-Legal* is released

15 July the European leg of the world tour concludes at Blackbushe aerodrome, Dylan playing to a huge audience of over 200,000, with Eric Clapton and other guests supporting

Autumn the American leg of the world tour takes place, to generally poorer reviews and audience reaction than the earlier concerts

24 November a sign of things to come: on stage Dylan wears a crucifix picked up at an earlier concert

1979

Spring Dylan is "born again".

May records the religious album *Slow Train Coming* at the Muscle Shoals studios in Alabama, produced by Jerry Wexler and Barry Beckett.

1 November first of a series of concerts where Dylan plays nothing but religious songs, to the dismay of many in the audiences

1980

January the religious concerts continue, Dylan delivering sermons from the stage to sometimes bewildered audiences

February wins Grammy award for the song "Gotta Serve Somebody"

November for the first time since his conversion, performs some older songs in concert alongside the newer religious material

1981

June-November another tour of Europe and North America with Dylan's old and new material mixed together

July Albert Grossman sues Dylan for over $1 million in their ongoing dispute

August *Shot Of Love* is released. Although still overtly religious in places, including the beautiful song "Every Grain of Sand", it also contains some secular material

1982

15 March Dylan is inducted to the Songwriters' Hall of Fame in New York

1983

11 April begins recording the *Infidels* album with Mark Knopfler producing

October the case between Dylan and his former manager Albert Grossman comes to court

1984

22 March Dylan makes an impressive live performance on the David Letterman show, backed by an LA punk band called the Cruzados

May-July Dylan tours Europe with Carlos Santana and (for a while) Joan Baez

1985

29 January Dylan participates in the recording of the "We Are The World" charity single, coached in his lyrics by Stevie Wonder

June *Empire Burlesque* is released

13 July Dylan is the final act on the bill at the Live Aid concert, backed by Keith Richards and Ronnie Wood of the Rolling Stones. The three may have taken some alcohol during rehearsals and the performance is not a success. "We came off looking like real idiots", was Wood's pithy summary of the event.

22 September performs, backed by Tom Petty and The Heartbreakers, at the Farm Aid concert

September participates in the recording of Steve Van Zandt's anti-apartheid single "Sun City"

13 November CBS throw a party to celebrate Dylan's twenty-five years in show business

December release of the *Biograph* boxed set of classic and rare performances

1986

25 January Dylan's former manager Albert Grossman dies of a heart attack on a flight from New York to London

February begins the True Confessions tour in New Zealand with Tom Petty and The Heartbreakers

4 March Richard Manuel, singer and piano player with The Band, commits suicide

4 June marries Carolyn Dennis, already mother of his daughter Desiree

August Dylan arrives in the UK to film *Hearts of Fire* directed by Richard Marquand

1987

11 March appears at a tribute evening for George Gershwin 50 years after the composer's death

5 September Dylan's first ever concert in Israel. The death of Richard Marquand, director of *Hearts of Fire*

19 September Dylan gives one of his most revealing interviews for the BBC *Omnibus* TV programme

9 October premiere of "Hearts Of Fire" in London. Dylan does not attend

1988

20 January Dylan is inducted into the Rock 'n' Roll Hall of Fame by Bruce Springsteen

April the Traveling Wilburys (as they are to become) gather at Dylan's house for

the first time to record music at Dylan's home studio

June Dylan begins a US tour with a three-piece backing band. This proves to be the start of the Never Ending Tour

4 December appears at Neil Young's annual Bridge Street benefit concert

7 December fellow Wilbury Roy Orbison dies from a heart attack

1989

March in New Orleans to record the *Oh Mercy* album produced by Daniel Lanois

May-November the Never Ending Tour continues

1990

January begins recording songs for *Under The Red Sky* produced by Don Was

30 January Dylan is in Paris, to be awarded by the French Minister of

Culture with the medal of Commandeur Des Arts Et Des Lettres

7 August Carolyn Dennis files for divorce from Dylan. The couple are officially divorced in 1992

17 September *Under The Red Sky* is released, to generally poor reviews. Dylan is not to release another album of original material until 1997

1991

20 February receives a Lifetime Achievement award at the Grammy Awards ceremony

March release of *The Bootleg Series Volumes I-III* containing, amongst other gems, the first official release of the Dylan classic song "Blind Willie McTell"

24 May Dylan's 50th birthday

1992

July-August at his home studio in Malibu Dylan records a selection of

traditional songs for *Good As I Been To You* alone on guitar and harmonica

18 October the Thirtieth Anniversary concert at Madison Square Garden. Dylan's career is celebrated by Neil Young, George Harrison, Eric Clapton, Lou Reed, Tom Petty, Roger McGuinn and many other artists performing versions of Dylan songs, before the star guest turns up to sing huskily through some of his greatest hits

1993

17 January sings at the Lincoln Memorial as part of the celebrations around Bill Clinton's inauguration as US president

May records the songs for *World Gone Wrong*. Once again, Dylan plays solo on guitar and harmonica and chooses to play covers of folk, blues and other traditional songs

16–17 November records two concerts at the intimate Supper Club in New York, intending to release a live TV

special of the shows. The project is abandoned, but the concerts themselves show Dylan in top form and bootlegs are coveted by fans

1994

5 February the latest leg of the Never Ending tour begins in Japan

20–22 May performs at The Great Music Experience in Japan, backed by a full orchestra. These performances are recorded for TV and, unusually for official TV appearances by Dylan, are both moving and accomplished

14 August performs at Woodstock II to an audience of 300,000, 25 years after he chose not to participate in the original concert

16–17 November Dylan and his band rehearse for and then record the MTV *Unplugged* show

1995

11 March the latest leg of the Never Ending Tour begins, in Prague, Czech Republic, with a particularly strong Dylan performance on vocals and, unusually, with the singer rarely using a guitar during the performance

19 November Dylan is part of an all-star cast at an 80th birthday concert for Frank Sinatra, performing a moving version of one of his early songs, "Restless Farewell"

1996

Autumn writing the songs that will later appear on *Time Out Of Mind*

1997

January begins recording *Time Out Of Mind* in Miami, Florida, produced by Daniel Lanois with whom Dylan had previously made 1989's *Oh Mercy*. The album is to prove Dylan's critical renaissance

5 April Allen Ginsberg, long-time friend and collaborator, dies of cancer

24 May Dylan's 56th birthday. At a family party he is taken ill with a rare and potentially fatal heart condition. "I really thought I'd be seeing Elvis soon", said Dylan of his brush with death

3 August returns to touring after some months of recuperation

27 September plays live for Pope John Paul II in Bologna

30 September release of the acclaimed *Time Out Of Mind* album

7 December receives the Kennedy Center medal from President Bill Clinton, who says of Dylan that "he probably had more impact on people of my generation than any other creative artist"

1998

25 February performs at the Grammy Awards and *Time Out Of Mind* wins in three categories

Summer tours North America and Europe with Van Morrison

October release of *The Bootleg Series Volume 4: Bob Dylan Live, 1966*. Although many have thought this classic live recording was made at the Royal Albert Hall it was actually from a concert in Manchester a few days earlier

1999

June-October tours the US with Paul Simon

2000

25 January Bob's mother Beatty dies of cancer aged 84

10 March the Never Ending Tour recommences

May "Things Have Changed" is released. It is part of the sound-track of the *Wonder Boys* film. It later wins both a Golden Globe and an Oscar

2001

11 September release of the album *Love And Theft* on the same day as the attack on the Twin Towers in New York. This is the second successive album of original material written by Dylan to achieve both commercial and critical success. Dylan's critical star has not been higher since the 1970s

30 November death of fellow Wilbury George Harrison from cancer

2002

Autumn the Never Ending Tour continues, with Dylan playing keyboards in preference to guitar, an approach he has taken ever since, rarely being seen playing the guitar on stage now

November Release of *Live 1975*, the latest in the Bootleg Series and a fine document of the Rolling Thunder Revue live sound

2003

15 July release of the *Masked and Anonymous* film, co-written by Dylan under a pseudonym. Dylan and his live band contribute some fine live performances to what is otherwise a rather unusual film, albeit with numerous big-name guest stars

2004

23 March release of *Live 1964*, another Bootleg Series release of a fine Dylan solo concert performance

October publication of *Chronicles Volume One*, Dylan's first volume of memoirs. The book is both critically well received and is a commercial success. An audio version, read by Sean Penn, is also successful

2005

21 July release of Martin Scorsese's acclaimed documentary *No Direction Home*. This focuses on Dylan between 1961 and 1966, culminating with the 1966 world tour, but including fascinating archive material and interviews with Dylan himself, Joan Baez, Suze Rotolo and many others whose lives Dylan touched

2006

3 May First broadcast of the *Theme Time Radio Hour* programme, featuring Dylan as the DJ and revealing a side to their hero that few fans would have predicted, Dylan proving an amiable and engaging host with diverse musical taste. The show seems set to continue into its third series and beyond

29 August release of the album *Modern Times*. This is seen as part of a trilogy

with the two previous albums of original material and yet again is well received by fans and critics alike

2007

August premiere of the movie *I'm Not There*, Todd Haynes' biographical film about Dylan, with different actors playing Dylan at different points in his career. Cate Blanchett delivers the best performance of the film with her impersonation of Dylan on the 1966 tour

1 October The compilation album *Dylan* is released by CBS, a three-disc set spanning Dylan's career, containing-both "greatest hits" and a trawl of some more obscure tracks

October paintings from Dylan's "Drawn Blank" series are exhibited in Germany. The exhibition moves to the UK the following year and demand for prints of Dylan's paintings is huge

2008

May Suze Rotolo publishes *A Freewheelin' Time*, her memoirs of life in New York with Dylan in the early 1960s

October *Tell Tale Signs* is the eighth volume in the Bootleg Series and collects unreleased and rare songs from the past 20 years of Dylan's career. It is voted one of the best albums of 2008

December The Never Ending Tour continues, with announcements of European dates for Dylan and his band between March and May 2009

Albums

BOB DYLAN
(COLUMBIA; MARCH 19, 1962)

You're No Good; Talkin' New York; In My Time Of Dyin'; Man Of Constant Sorrow; Fixin' To Die; Pretty Peggy-O; Highway 51 Blues; Gospel Plow; Baby, Let Me Follow You Down; House Of The Risin' Sun; Freight Train Blues; Song To Woody; See That My Grave Is Kept Clean

THE FREEWHEELIN' BOB DYLAN
(COLUMBIA; MAY 27, 1963)

Blowin' In The Wind; Girl From The North Country; Masters Of War; Down The Highway; Bob Dylan's Blues; A Hard Rain's A-Gonna Fall; Don't Think Twice, It's All Right; Bob Dylan's Dream; Oxford Town; Talking World War III Blues; Corrina, Corrina; Honey, Just Allow Me One More Chance; I Shall Be Free (Some extremely rare copies of the original pressing of this album also contained Talkin' John Birch Paranoid Blues; Rambling, Gambling Willie; Rocks & Gravel (aka Solid Road); Let Me Die in My Footsteps)

THE TIMES THEY ARE A-CHANGIN'
(COLUMBIA; JANUARY 13. 1964)

The Times They Are A-Changin'; Ballad Of Hollis Brown; With God On Our Side; One Too Many Mornings; North Country Blues; Only A Pawn In Their Game; Boots Of Spanish Leather; When The Ship Comes In; The Lonesome Death Of Hattie Carroll; Restless Farewell

ANOTHER SIDE OF BOB DYLAN
(COLUMBIA; AUGUST 8, 1964)

All I Really Want To Do; Black Crow Blues; Spanish Harlem Incident; Chimes Of Freedom; I Shall Be Free No. 10; To Ramona; Motorpsycho Nitemare; My Back Pages; I Don't Believe You (She Acts Like We Never Have Met); Ballad In Plain D; It Ain't Me Babe

BRINGING IT ALL BACK HOME
(COLUMBIA; MARCH 22, 1965)

Subterranean Homesick Blues; She Belongs To Me; Maggie's Farm, Love Minus Zero/No Limit; Outlaw Blues; On The Road Again; Bob Dylan's 115th Dream; Mr. Tambourine Man; Gates Of Eden; It's Alright, Ma (I'm Only Bleeding); It's All Over Now, Baby Blue

HIGHWAY 61 REVISITED
(COLUMBIA; AUGUST 30, 1965)

Like A Rolling Stone; Tombstone Blues; It Takes A Lot To Laugh, It Takes A Train To Cry; From A Buick 6; Ballad Of A Thin Man; Queen Jane Approximately; Highway 61 Revisited; Just Like Tom Thumb's Blues; Desolation Row

BLONDE ON BLONDE
(COLUMBIA; MAY 16, 1966)

Rainy Day Women #12 & 35; Pledging My Time; Visions Of Johanna; One Of Us Must Know (Sooner Or Later); I Want You; Stuck Inside Of Mobile With The Memphis Blues Again; Leopard-Skin Pill-Box Hat; Just Like A Woman; Most Likely You Go Your Way (And I'll Go Mine); Temporary Like Achilles; Absolutely Sweet Marie; 4th Time Around; Obviously 5 Believers; Sad Eyed Lady Of The Lowlands

BOB DYLAN'S GREATEST HITS
(COLUMBIA; MARCH 27, 1967)

Rainy Day Women #12 & 35; Blowin' In The Wind; The Times They Are A-Changin'; It Ain't Me Babe; Like A Rolling Stone; Mr. Tambourine Man; Subterranean Homesick Blues; I Want You; Positively 4th Street; Just Like A Woman

JOHN WESLEY HARDING
(COLUMBIA; DECEMBER 27, 1967)

John Wesley Harding; As I Went Out One Morning; I Dreamed I Saw St. Augustine; All Along The Watchtower; The Ballad Of Frankie Lee And Judas Priest; Drifter's Escape; Dear Landlord; I Am A Lonesome Hobo; I Pity The Poor Immigrant; The Wicked Messenger; Down Along The Cove; I'll Be Your Baby Tonight

NASHVILLE SKYLINE
(COLUMBIA; APRIL 9, 1969)

Girl From The North Country; Nashville Skyline Rag; To Be Alone With You; I Threw It All Away; Peggy Day; Lay Lady Lay; One More Night; Tell Me That It Isn't True; Country Pie; Tonight I'll Be Staying Here With You

SELF PORTRAIT
(COLUMBIA; JUNE 8, 1970)

All The Tired Horses; Alberta #1; I Forgot More Than You'll Ever Know; Days Of '49; Early Mornin' Rain; In Search Of Little Sadie; Let It Be Me; Little Sadie; Woogie Boogie; Belle Isle; Living The Blues; Like A Rolling Stone; Copper Kettle; Gotta Travel On; Blue Moon; The Boxer; The Might Quinn (Quinn The Eskimo); Take Me As I Am (Or Let Me Go); Take A Message To Mary; It Hurts Me Too; Minstrel Boy; She Belongs To Me; Wigwam; Alberta #2

NEW MORNING
(COLUMBIA; OCTOBER 19, 1970)

If Not For You; Day Of The Locusts; Time Passes Slowly; Went To See The Gypsy; Winterlude; If Dogs Run Free; New Morning; Sign On The Window; One More Weekend; The Man In Me; Three Angels; Father Of Night

BOB DYLAN'S GREATEST HITS VOL II/MORE BOB DYLAN GREATEST HITS (COLUMBIA; NOVEMBER 17, 1971)
Disc 1

Watching The River Flow; Don't Think Twice, It's All Right; Lay Lady Lay; Stuck Inside Of Mobile With The Memphis Blues Again; I'll Be Your Baby Tonight; All I Really Want To Do; My Back Pages; Maggie's Farm; Tonight I'll Be Staying Here With You

Disc 2

She Belongs To Me; All Along The Watchtower; The Mighty Quinn (Quinn The Eskimo); Just Like Tom Thumb's Blues; A Hard Rain's A-Gonna Fall; If Not For You; It's All Over Now, Baby Blue; Tomorrow Is A Long Time; When I Paint My Masterpiece; I Shall Be Released; You Ain't Goin' Nowhere; Down In The Flood

PAT GARRETT & BILLY THE KID (COLUMBIA; JULY 16, 1973)

Main Title Theme (Billy); Cantina Theme (Workin' For The Law); Billy 1; Bunkhouse Theme; River Theme; Turkey Chase; Knockin' On Heaven's Door; Final Theme; Billy 4; Billy 7

DYLAN (COLUMBIA; NOVEMBER 19, 1973)

Lily Of The West; Can't Help Falling In Love; Sarah Jane; The Ballad Of Ira Hayes; Mr. Bojangles; Mary Ann; Big Yellow Taxi; A Fool Such As I; Spanish Is The Loving Tongue

PLANET WAVES (ASYLUM; JANUARY 17, 1974)

On A Night Like This; Going, Going, Gone; Tough Mama; Hazel; Something There Is About You; Forever Young; Forever Young (Continued); Dirge; You Angel You; Never Say Goodbye; Wedding Song

BEFORE THE FLOOD (ASYLUM/COLUMBIA; JUNE 20, 1974)
Disc 1

Most Likely You Go Your Way (And I'll Go Mine); Lay Lady Lay; Rainy Day Women #12 & 35; Knockin' On Heaven's Door; It Ain't Me Babe; Ballad Of A Thin Man; Up On Cripple Creek; I Shall Be Released; Endless Highway; The Night They Drove Old Dixie Down; Stage Fright;

Disc 2

Don't Think Twice; It's All Right; Just Like A Woman; It's Alright, Ma (I'm Only Bleeding); Shape I'm In; When You Awake; Weight; All Along The Watchtower; Highway 61 Revisited; Like A Rolling Stone; Blowin' In The Wind

BLOOD ON THE TRACKS (COLUMBIA; JANUARY 17, 1975)

Tangled Up In Blue; Simple Twist Of Fate; You're A Big Girl Now; Idiot Wind; You're Gonna Make Me Lonesome When You Go; Meet Me In The Morning; Lily Rosemary And The Jack Of Hearts; If You See Her, Say Hello; Shelter From The Storm; Buckets Of Rain

THE BASEMENT TAPES (COLUMBIA; JUNE 26, 1975)

Odds And Ends; Orange Juice Blues (Blues For Breakfast), Million Dollar Bash, Yazoo Street Scandal, Goin' To Acapulco, Katie's Been Gone, Lo And Behold!, Bessie Smith, Clothes Line Saga, Apple Suckling Tree, Please Mrs. Henry, Tears Of Rage, Too Much Of Nothing, Yea! Heavy And A Bottle Of Bread, Ain't No More Cane, Crash on The Levee, Ruben Remus, Tiny Montgomery, You Ain't Goin' Nowhere, Don't Ya Tell Henry, Nothing Was Delivered, Open The Door, Homer, Long Distance Operator, This Wheel's On Fire)

DESIRE (COLUMBIA; JANUARY 5, 1976)

Hurricane; Isis; Mozambique; One More Cup Of Coffee (Valley Below); Oh, Sister; Joey; Romance In Durango; Black Diamond Bay; Sara

HARD RAIN (COLUMBIA; SEPTEMBER 13, 1976)

Maggie's Farm; One Too Many Mornings; Stuck Inside Of Mobile With The Memphis Blues Again; Oh Sister; Lay Lady Lay; Shelter From The Storm; You're A Big Girl Now; I Threw It All Away; Idiot Wind

MASTERPIECES (COLUMBIA; MARCH 1978 IN AUSTRALIA, NEW ZEALAND & JAPAN ONLY)
Disc 1

Knockin' On Heaven's Door; Mr. Tambourine Man; Just Like A Woman; I Shall Be Released; Tears Of Rage; All Along The Watchtower; One More Cup Of Coffee (Valley Below); Like A Rolling Stone; The Mighty Quinn; Tomorrow Is A Long Time; Lay Lady Lay; Idiot Wind

Disc 2

Mixed Up Confusion; Positively 4th Street; Can You Please Crawl Out Your Window?; Just Like Tom Thumb's Blues; Spanish Is The Loving Tongue; George Jackson; Rita May; Blowin' In The Wind; A Hard Rain's A-Gonna Fall; The Times They Are A Changin'; Masters Of War; Hurricane

Disc 3

Maggie's Farm; Subterranean Homesick Blues; Ballad Of A Thin Man; Mozambique; This Wheel's On Fire; I Want You; Rainy Day Woman # 12 & 35; Don't Think Twice; It's Alright; Song To Woody; It Ain't Me Babe; Love Minus Zero/No Limit; I'll Be Your Baby Tonight; If Not For You; If You See Her Say Hello; Sara

STREET LEGAL (COLUMBIA; JUNE 15, 1978)

Changing Of The Guards; New Pony; No Time To Think; Baby Stop Crying; Is Your Love In Vain?; Señor (Tales of Yankee Power); True Love Tends To Forget; We Better Talk This Over; Where Are You Tonight (Journey Through Dark Heat)

BOB DYLAN AT BUDOKAN (COLUMBIA; APRIL 23 1979)
Disc 1

Mr. Tambourine Man; Shelter From The Storm; Love Minus Zero/No Limit; Ballad Of A Thin Man; Don't Think Twice, It's All Right;

Maggie's Farm; One More Cup Of Coffee (Valley Below); Like A Rolling Stone; I Shall Be Released; Is Your Love In Vain?; Going, Going, Gone

Disc 2

Blowin' In The Wind; Just Like A Woman; Oh, Sister; Simple Twist Of Fate; All Along The Watchtower; I Want You; All I Really Want To Do; Knockin' On Heaven's Door; It's Alright Ma (I'm only Bleeding); Forever Young; The Times They Are A-Changin'

SLOW TRAIN COMING
(COLUMBIA, AUGUST 20, 1979)

Gotta Serve Somebody; Precious Angel; I Believe In You; Slow Train; Gonna Change My Way Of Thinking; Do Right To Me Baby (Do Unto Others); When You Gonna Wake Up; Man Gave Name To All The Animals; When He Returns

SAVED
(COLUMBIA; JUNE 23, 1980)

A Satisfied Mind; Saved; Covenant Woman; What Can I Do For You?; Solid Rock; Pressing On; In The Garden; Saving Grace; Are You Ready

SHOT OF LOVE
(COLUMBIA; AUGUST 10, 1981)

Shot Of Love; Heart Of Mine; Property Of Jesus; Lenny Bruce; Watered-Down Love; Dead Man, Dead Man; In The Summertime; Trouble; Every Grain Of Sand (The Groom's Still Waiting At The Altar was added as track 6 when this album was re-released in 1985)

INFIDELS
(COLUMBIA; OCTOBER 27, 1983)

Jokerman; Sweetheart Like You; Neighborhood Bully; License To Kill; Man Of Peace; Union Sundown; I & I; Don't Fall Apart On Me Tonight

REAL LIVE
(COLUMBIA; DECEMBER 3, 1984)

Highway 61 Revisited; Maggie's Farm; I & I; License To Kill; It Ain't Me Babe; Tangled Up In Blue; Masters Of War; Ballad Of A Thin Man; Girl From The North Country; Tombstone Blues

EMPIRE BURLESQUE
(COLUMBIA; JUNE 10, 1985)

Tight Connection To My Heart (Has Anybody Seen My Love); Seeing The Real You At Last; I'll Remember You; Clean Cut Kid; Never Gonna Be The Same Again; Trust Yourself; Emotionally Yours; When The Night Comes Falling From The Sky; Something's Burning, Baby; Dark Eyes

BIOGRAPH
(COLOMBIA; NOVEMBER 7, 1985)
Disc 1

Lay Lady Lay; Baby, Let Me Follow You Down; If Not For You, I'll Be Your Baby Tonight; I'll Keep It With Mine; The Times They Are A-Changin'; Blowin' In The Wind; Masters Of War; The Lonesome Death Of Hattie Carroll; Percy's Song; Mixed-Up Confusion; Tombstone Blues; The Groom's Still Waiting At The Altar; Most Likely You Go Your Way (And I'll Go Mine); Like A Rolling Stone; Lay

Down Your Weary Tune; Subterranean Homesick Blues; I Don't Believe You (She Acts Like We Never Have Met)

Disc 2

Visions Of Johanna; Every Grain Of Sand; Quinn The Eskimo (The Mighty Quinn); Mr. Tambourine Man; Dear Landlord; It Ain't Me, Babe; You Angel You; Million Dollar Bash; To Ramona; You're A Big Girl Now; Abandoned Love; Tangled Up In Blue; It's All Over Now, Baby Blue; Can You Please Crawl Out Your Window?; Positively 4th Street; Isis; Jet Pilot

Disc 3

Caribbean Wind; Up To Me; Baby, I'm In The Mood For You; I Wanna Be Your Lover; I Want You; Heart Of Mine; On A Night Like This; Just Like A Woman; Romance In Durango; Señor (Tales of Yankee Power); Gotta Serve Somebody; I Believe In You; Time Passes Slowly; I Shall Be Released; Knockin' On Heaven's Door; All Along The Watchtower; Solid Rock; Forever Young

KNOCKED OUT LOADED
(COLUMBIA; JULY 14, 1986)

You Wanna Ramble; They Killed Him; Driftin' Too Far From Shore; Precious Memories; Maybe Someday; Brownsville Girl; Got My Mind Made Up; Under Your Spell

DOWN IN THE GROOVE
(COLUMBIA; MAY 30, 1988)

Let's Stick Together; When Did You Leave Heaven?; Sally Sue Brown; Death Is Not The End; Had A

Dream About You, Baby; Ugliest Girl In The World; Silvio; Ninety Miles An Hour (Down A Dead End Street); Shenandoah; Rank Strangers To Me

DYLAN & THE DEAD
(COLUMBIA; JANUARY 30, 1989)

Slow Train; I Want You; Gotta Serve Somebody; Queen Jane Approximately; Joey; All Along The Watchtower; Knockin' On Heaven's Door

OH MERCY
(COLUMBIA; SEPTEMBER 18, 1989)

Political World; Where Teardrops Fall; Everything Is Broken; Ring Them Bells; Man In The Long Black Coat; Most Of The Time; What Good Am I?; Disease Of Conceit; What Was It You Wanted; Shooting Star

UNDER THE RED SKY
(COLUMBIA; SEPTEMBER 10, 1990)

Wiggle Wiggle; Under The Red Sky; Unbelievable; Born In Time; T.V. Talkin' Song; 10,000 Men; 2 X 2; God Knows; Handy Dandy; Cat's In The Well

THE BOOTLEG SERIES, VOLUMES 1–3 (RARE AND UNRELEASED 1961–1991)
(COLUMBIA; MARCH 26, 1991)
Disc 1

Hard Times In New York Town; He Was A Friend Of Mine; Man On The Street; No More Auction Block; House Carpenter; Talkin' Bear Mountain Picnic Massacre Blues; Let Me Die In My Footsteps;

Rambling, Gambling Willie; Talkin' Hava Negeilah Blues; Quit Your Low Down Ways; Worried Blues; Kingsport Town; Walkin' Down The Line; Walls Of Red Wing; Paths Of Victory; Talkin' John Birch Paranoid Blues; Who Killed Davey Moore?; Only A Hobo; Moonshiner; When The Ship Comes In; The Times They Are A-Changin'; Last Thoughts On Woody Guthrie

Disc 2

Seven Curses; Eternal Circle; Suze (The Cough Song); Mama, You Been On My Mind; Farewell, Angelina; Subterranean Homesick Blues; If You Gotta Go, Go Now (Or Else You Got to Stay All Night); Sitting On A Barbed Wire Fence; Like A Rolling Stone; It Takes A Lot To Laugh, It Takes A Train To Cry; I'll Keep It With Mine; She's Your Lover Now; I Shall Be Released; Santa-Fe; If Not For You; Wallflower; Nobody 'Cept You; Tangled Up In Blue; Call Letter Blues; Idiot Wind

Disc 3

If You See Her Say Hello; Golden Loom; Catfish; Seven Days; Ye Shall Be Changed; Every Grain Of Sand; You Changed My Life; Need A Woman; Angelina; Someone's Got A Hold Of My Heart; Tell Me; Lord Protect My Child; Foot Of Pride; Blind Willie McTell; When The Night Comes Falling From The Sky; Series Of Dreams

GOOD AS I BEEN TO YOU
(COLUMBIA; NOVEMBER 3, 1992)

Frankie & Albert; Jim Jones; Blackjack Davey; Canadee-I-O; Sittin' On Top Of The World; Little Maggie; Hard Times; Step It Up And Go; Tomorrow Night; Arthur McBride; You're Gonna Quit Me; Diamond Joe; Froggie Went A Courtin'

WORLD GONE WRONG
(COLUMBIA, 1993)

World Gone Wrong; Love Henry; Ragged & Dirty; Blood In My Eyes; Broke Down Engine; Delia; Stack A Lee; Two Soldiers; Jack-A-Roe; Lone Pilgrim

BOB DYLAN'S GREATEST HITS VOLUME 3
(COLUMBIA; NOVEMBER 15, 1994)

Tangled Up In Blue; Changing Of The Guards; The Groom's Still Waiting At The Altar; Hurricane; Forever Young; Jokerman; Dignity; Silvio; Ring Them Bells; Gotta Serve Somebody; Series Of Dreams; Brownsville Girl; Under The Red Sky; Knockin' On Heaven's Door

MTV UNPLUGGED
(COLUMBIA; MAY 2, 1995)

Tombstone Blues; Shooting Star; All Along The Watchtower; The Times They Are A-Changin'; John Brown; Desolation Row; Rainy Day Women #12 & 35; Dignity; Knockin' On Heaven's Door; Like A Rolling Stone; With God On Our Side

THE BOOTLEG SERIES, VOLUME 4 (BOB DYLAN LIVE, 1966: THE ROYAL ALBERT HALL CONCERT) (COLUMBIA; OCTOBER 13, 1998)
Disc 1

She Belongs To Me; Fourth Time Around; Visions Of Johanna; It's All Over Now, Baby Blue; Desolation Row; Just Like A Woman; Mr. Tambourine Man

Disc 2

Tell Me, Momma; I Don't Believe You (She Acts Like We Never Have Met); Baby, Let Me Follow You Down; Just Like Tom Thumb's Blues; Leopard-Skin Pill-Box Hat; One Too Many Mornings; Ballad Of A Thin Man; Like A Rolling Stone

TIME OUT OF MIND
(COLUMBIA; SEPTEMBER 30, 1997)

Love Sick; Dirt Road Blues; Standing In The Doorway; Million Miles; Tryin' To Get To Heaven; 'Til I Fell In Love With You; Not Dark Yet; Cold Irons Bound; Make You Feel My Love; Can't Wait; Highlands

THE ESSENTIAL BOB DYLAN
(COLUMBIA; OCTOBER 31, 2000)
Disc 1

Blowin' In The Wind; Don't Think Twice, It's All Right; The Times They Are A-Changin'; It Ain't Me Babe; Maggie's Farm; It's All Over Now, Baby Blue; Mr. Tambourine Man; Subterranean Homesick Blues; Like A Rolling Stone; Positively 4th Street; Just Like A Woman; Rainy Day Women #12 & 35; All Along The Watchtower; Quinn The Eskimo (The Mighty Quinn); I'll Be Your Baby Tonight

Disc 2

Lay Lady Lay; If Not For You; I Shall Be Released; You Ain't Going Nowhere; Knockin' On Heaven's Door; Forever Young; Tangled Up In Blue; Shelter From The Storm; Hurricane; Gotta Serve Somebody; Jokerman; Silvio; Everything Is Broken; Not Dark Yet; Things Have Changed

THE ESSENTIAL BOB DYLAN
(COLUMBIA; 2001 IN AUSTRALIA AND NEW ZEALAND ONLY)
Disc 1

Blowin' In The Wind; Don't Think Twice, It's All Right; The Times They Are A Changin'; It Ain't Me Babe; Maggie's Farm; It's All Over Now, Baby Blue; Mr. Tambourine Man; Subterranean Homesick Blues; Like A Rolling Stone; Positively 4th Street; I Want You; Just Like A Woman; Rainy Day Women #12 & 35; All Along The Watchtower; I'll Be Your Baby Tonight; Lay, Lady Lay; If Not For You; I Shall Be Released; Knockin' On Heaven's Door

Disc 2

Forever Young; Tangled Up In Blue; Shelter From The Storm; Hurricane; Changing Of The Guards; Gotta Serve Somebody; Blind Willie McTell; Jokerman; Tight Connection To My Heart (Has Anybody Seen My Love?); Everything Is Broken; Dignity; Not Dark Yet; Things Have Changed

LIVE 1961-2000; THIRTY-NINE YEARS OF GREAT CONCERT PERFORMANCES (SME; FEBRUARY 28, 2001 IN JAPAN ONLY)

Somebody Touched Me; Wade In The Water; Handsome Molly; To Ramona; I Don't Believe You (She Acts Like We Never Have Met); Grand Coulee Dam; Knockin' On Heaven's Door; It Ain't Me, Babe; Shelter From The Storm; Dead Man, Dead Man; Slow Train; Dignity; Cold Irons Bound; Born In Time; Country Pie; Things Have Changed

"LOVE AND THEFT" (SONY, SEPTEMBER 11, 2001)

Tweedle Dee & Tweedle Dum; Mississippi; Summer Days; Bye And Bye; Lonesome Day Blues; Floater (Too Much To Ask); High Water (for Charlie Patton); Moonlight; Honest With Me; Po' Boy; Cry A While; Sugar Baby

THE BOOTLEG SERIES, VOLUME 5 (BOB DYLAN LIVE, 1975: THE ROLLING THUNDER REVUE) (COLUMBIA; NOVEMBER 26, 2002) Disc 1

Tonight I'll Be Staying Here With You; It Ain't Me Babe; A Hard Rain's-A-Gonna Fall; The Lonesome Death Of Hattie Carroll; Romance In Durango; Isis; Mr. Tambourine Man; Simple Twist Of Fate; Blowin' In The Wind; Mama, You Been On My Mind; I Shall Be Released

Disc 2

It's All Over Now, Baby Blue; Love Minus Zero/No Limit; Tangled Up In Blue; The Water Is Wide; It Takes A Lot To Laugh, It Takes A Train To Cry; Oh, Sister; Hurricane; One More Cup Of Coffee (Valley Below); Sara; Just Like A Woman; Knockin' On Heaven's Door

THE BOOTLEG SERIES, VOLUME 6 (BOB DYLAN LIVE, 1964: CONCERT AT PHILHARMONIC HALL) (COLUMBIA; MARCH 30, 2004) Disc 1

The Times They Are A-Changin'; Spanish Harlem Incident; Talkin' John Birch Paranoid Blues; To Ramona; Who Killed Davey Moore; Gates of Eden; If You Gotta Go, Go Now (Or Else You Got To Stay All Night); It's Alright, Ma (I'm Only Bleeding); I Don't Believe You (She Acts Like We Never Have Met); Mr. Tambourine Man; A Hard Rain's-A-Gonna Fall

Disc 2

Talkin' World War III Blues; Don't Think Twice, It's All Right; The Lonesome Death Of Hattie Carroll; Mama, You Been On My Mind; Silver Dagger; With God On Our Side; It Ain't Me, Babe; All I Really Want To Do

THE BOOTLEG SERIES, VOLUME 7 (NO DIRECTION HOME: THE SOUNDTRACK) (COLUMBIA; AUGUST 30, 2005) Disc 1

When I Got Troubles; Rambler, Gambler; This Land Is Your Land; Song To Woody; Dink's Song; I Was Young When I Left Home; Sally Gal; Don't Think Twice, It's All Right; Man Of Constant Sorrow; Blowin' In The Wind; Masters Of War; A Hard Rain's-A-Gonna Fall; When The Ship Comes In; Mr. Tambourine Man; Chimes Of Freedom; It's All Over Now, Baby Blue

Disc 2

She Belongs To Me; Maggie's Farm; It Takes A Lot To Laugh, It Takes A Train To Cry; Tombstone Blues; Just Like Tom Thumb's Blues; Desolation Row; Highway 61 Revisited; Leopard-Skin Pill-Box Hat; Stuck Inside Of Mobile With The Memphis Blues Again; Visions Of Johanna; Ballad Of A Thin Man; Like A Rolling Stone

LIVE AT THE GASLIGHT 1962 (COLUMBIA; AUGUST 30, 2005)

A Hard Rain's-A-Gonna Fall; Rocks and Gravel; Don't Think Twice, It's All Right; The Cuckoo (Is A Pretty Bird); Moonshiner; Handsome Molly; Cocaine; John Brown; Barbara Allen; West Texas

THE BEST OF BOB DYLAN (COLUMBIA; NOVEMBER 15, 2005)

Blowin' In The Wind; The Times They Are A-Changin'; Mr. Tambourine Man; Like A Rolling Stone; Rainy Day Women #12 & 35; All Along The Watchtower; Lay Lady Lay; Knockin' On Heaven's Door; Tangled Up In Blue; Hurricane; Forever Young; Gotta Serve Somebody; Jokerman; Not Dark Yet; Things Have Changed; Summer Days

BOB DYLAN BLUES (COLUMBIA; AUGUST 8, 2006)

She Belongs To Me; Leopard-Skin Pill-Box Hat; It Takes A Lot To Laugh, It Takes A Train To Cry; Down In The Flood; Meet Me In The Morning; Gotta Serve Somebody; The Groom's Still Waiting at the Altar; Seeing The Real You At Last; Everything Is Broken; Dirt Road Blues; High Water (For Charley Patton); Blind Willie McTell

MODERN TIMES (SONY; AUGUST 29, 2006)

Thunder On The Mountain; Spirit On The Water; Rollin' And Tumblin'; When The Deal Goes Down; Someday Baby; Workingman's Blues; Beyond The Horizon; Nettie Moore; The Levee's Gonna Break; Ain't Talkin'

DYLAN (COLUMBIA; OCTOBER 1, 2007) Single Disc Edition

Blowin' In The Wind; The Times They Are A-Changing; Subterranean Homesick Blues; Mr. Tambourine Man; Like A Rolling Stone; Maggie's Farm; Positively 4th Street; Just Like A Woman; Rainy Day Women #12 & 35; All Along The Watchtower; Lay Lady Lay; Knockin' On Heaven's Door; Tangled Up In Blue; Hurricane; Make You Feel My Love; Things Have Changed; Someday Baby; Forever Young

Three-Disc Edition Disc 1

Song To Woody; Blowin' In The Wind; Masters Of War; Don't Think Twice, It's All Right; A Hard Rain's

A-Gonna Fall; The Times They Are A-Changing; All I really Want To Do; My Back Pages; It Ain't Me, Babe; Subterranean Homesick Blues; Mr. Tambourine Man; Maggie's Farm; Like A Rolling Stone; It's All Over Now, Baby Blue; Positively 4th Street; Rainy Day Women #12 & 35; Just Like A Woman; Most Likely You Go Your Way (And I'll Go Mine); All Along The Watchtower

Three-Disc Edition Disc 2

You Ain't Going Nowhere; Lay Lady Lay; If Not For You; I Shall Be Released; Knockin' On Heaven's Door; On A Night Like This; Forever Young; Tangled Up In Blue; Simple Twist Of Fate; Hurricane; Changing Of The Guards; Gotta Serve Somebody; Precious Angel; The Groom's Still Waiting At The Altar; Jokerman; Dark Eyes

Three-Disc Edition Disc 3

Blind Willie McTell; Brownsville Girl; Silvio; Ring Them Bells; Dignity; Everything Is Broken; Under The Red Sky; You're Gonna Quit Me; Blood In My Eyes; Not Dark Yet; Things Have Changed; Make You Feel My Love; High Water (For Charley Patton); Po' Boy; Someday Baby; When The Deal Goes Down

THE BOOTLEG SERIES, VOLUME 8 (TELL TALE SIGNS: RARE AND UNRELEASED 1989–2006) (COLUMBIA; OCTOBER 6, 2008)

Disc 1

Mississippi (Alternate version 1); Most Of The Time; Dignity; Someday Baby; Red River Shore; Tell Ol' Bill; Born In Time; Can't Wait; Everything Is Broken; Dreamin' Of You; Huck's Tune; Marchin' To The City; High Water (For Charley Patton)

Disc 2

Mississippi (Alternate version 2); 32–20 Blues; Series Of Dreams; God Knows; Can't Escape From You; Dignity; Ring Them Bells; Cocaine Blues; Ain't Talkin'; The Girl On The Greenbriar Shore; Lonesome Day Blues; Miss The Mississippi; The Lonesome River; 'Cross The Green Mountain

Singles

1962

Mixed Up Confusion/Corrina Corrina

1963

Blowin' In The Wind/Don't Think Twice, It's All Right

1964

The Times They Are A Changin'/Honey, Just Allow Me
    One More Chance

1965

Subterranean Homesick Blues/She Belongs To Me

Maggie's Farm/On The Road Again

Like A Rolling Stone Part 1 & 2/ Gates Of Eden

Positively 4th Street/From A Buick 6Highway 61 Revisited/Can You
    Please Crawl Out Your Window UK only)

1966

Queen Jane Approximately/One Of Us Must Know

Rainy Day Women #12 & 35/Pledging My Time

I Want You/Just like Tom Thumb's Blues

Leopard-skin Pill-box Hat/Most Likely You Go Your Way (And
    I'll Go Mine)

Just Like A Woman/Only Five Believers

1967

If You Gotta Go, Go Now (Or Else You Got To Stay All Night/To
    Ramona

1968

All Along The Watchtower/I'll Be Your Baby Tonight

1969

I Threw It All Away/Drifter's EscapeLay Lady Lay/Peggy Day

Tonight I'll Be Staying Here With You/Country Pie

1970

Wigwam/Copper Kettle

1971

If Not For You/New Morning Watching The River Flow/New Morning

George Jackson/George Jackson (acoustic)

1973

Knockin' On Heaven's Door/Turkey Chase

1974

A Fool Such As I/Lily Of The West

On A Night Like This/You Angel You

Something There Is About You/Tough Mama

Most Likely You Go Your Way (And I'll Go Mine) (live)/Stage Fright

It Ain't Me Babe (live)/All Along The Watchtower (live)

1975

Tangled Up In Blue/If You See, Say Hello

Million Dollar Bash/Tears Of Rage

Hurricane Parts 1 & 2

Mozambique/Oh Sister

1976

Stuck Inside Of Mobile With The Memphis Blues Again/Rita May

1978

Baby Stop Crying/We Better Talk This Over

Changing Of The Guard/Senor (UK only)

1979

Man Gave Names To All the Animals/When You Gonna Wake Up?

Gotta Serve Somebody/Trouble In Mind (1979)

1980

Slow Train/Do Right To Me Baby

Solid Rock/Covenant Woman

Saved/Are You Ready

1981

Heart Of Mine/Let It Be Me

Dead Man, Dead Man/Lenny Bruce

1983

Union Sundown/Angels Flying Too Close To The Ground

1984

Jokerman/Isis

1985

Tight Connection To My Heart/We Better Talk This Over

Emotionally Yours/When The Night Comes Falling From The Sky

1986

Band Of The Band/Theme Joe's Death (not Dylan)

The Usual/Got My Mind Made Up (UK Only)

1988

Silvio/Driftin' Too Far From Shore

1989

Everything Is Broken/Death Is Not the End

1990

Political World

Unbelievable

1991

Series Of Dreams

Blind Willie McTell

1993

My Back Pages

1994

Dignity

1995

Dignity MTV Unplugged

Knockin' On Heaven's Door MTV Unplugged

1997

Rock & Folk Le Sampler

1998

Love Sick CD 1

Love Sick CD 2

Not Dark Yet

Not Dark Yet Vol. 2

2000

Things Have Changed

2004

Went To See The Gypsy (iTunes Music Store)

2005

Exclusive Outtakes From No Direction Home: The Soundtrack

(iTunes Music Store)

Acknowledgements

The publishers would like to thank the following libraries and photographers for their kind permission to reproduce their photographs in this book.

Getty images: 9, 10, 11, 12, 13, 14, 15, 16, 17, 18, 19, 20, 21, 22, 23, 24, 25, 26, 27, 28, 29, 30, 31, 32, 33, 34, 35, 36, 37, 38, 39, 40, 41, 42, 43, 44, 45, 46, 47, 48, 49, 50, 5156, 57, 58, 59, 60, 61, 62, 63, 64, 65. 66, 67, 68, 69. 70, 71, 72, 73, 80 , 81, 82, 83, 84, 85, 90, 91, 95, 96, 98, 99, 100, 101, 102, 103, 104, 105, 106, 107, 108, 109, 110, 111, 112, 113, 114, 115, 116, 117, 118, 119, 120, 121, 122, 123, 124, 125, 126, 127, 128, 129, 132, 133, 134. 135 136, 137, 138, 139, 140, 141,142, 143, 144, 145, 146, 147, 148, 149, 150, 151, 152, 153,154, 166, 158, 159, 160, 161, 162, 163, 164, 165, 166, 167, 168, 169, 170, 171, 172, 173, 174, 175, 176, 178, 179, 180, 181, 182, 183, 184, 185, 186, 188, 189, 190, 191, 192, 193, 194, 195, 196, 197, 198, 199, 200, 201, 202, 203, 205

Redferns Music Picture Library: Douglas R. Gilbert; 52, 53, 54, 55; Jan Persson 74, 75, 76, 77, 78, 79; Elliott Landy 86, 87, 88, 89, 92, 93; Fotex Agentur 156; Fotex/Herbert Kueln 157,

Corbis: 97, 130, 131,170, 187

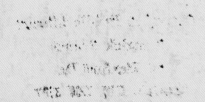